A | Pre-View
of Policy
Sciences

Policy Sciences Book Series

A Series of Studies, Textbooks, and Reference Works

Edited by YEHEZKEL DROR

Hebrew University of Jerusalem

PUBLISHED

Yehezkel Dror
Design for Policy Sciences, 1971

Yehezkel Dror
Ventures in Policy Sciences, 1971

Harold D. Lasswell
A Pre-View of Policy Sciences, 1971

Beatrice K. Rome and Sydney C. Rome
Organizational Growth through Decisionmaking, 1971

Walter Williams
Social Policy Research and Analysis, 1971

IN PREPARATION

Benson D. Adams
Ballistic Missile Defense

Joseph P. Martino
Technological Forecasting for Decisionmaking

A Pre-View of Policy Sciences

Harold D. Lasswell

Professor of Policy Sciences
John Jay College of Criminal Justice
The City University of New York

Ford Foundation Professor Emeritus
of Law and Social Sciences
Yale University Law School
New Haven, Connecticut

American Elsevier
Publishing Company, Inc.
NEW YORK

AMERICAN ELSEVIER PUBLISHING COMPANY, INC.
52 Vanderbilt Avenue, New York, N.Y. 10017

ELSEVIER PUBLISHING COMPANY, LTD.
Barking, Essex, England

ELSEVIER PUBLISHING COMPANY
335 Jan Van Galenstraat, P.O. Box 211
Amsterdam, The Netherlands

International Standard Book Number 0-444-00112-3

Library of Congress Card Number 78-165801

Manufactured in the United States of America

Contents

Series Editor's Introductory Note xi
Preface xiii

CHAPTER 1

The Evolution of the Policy Sciences **1**

A Working Definition 1
Policy Science Careers 4
Historical Trends 9

CHAPTER 2

Contextuality: Mapping the Social and Decision Processes **14**

Introduction 14
A Social Process Model 15
A Decision Process Model 27

CHAPTER 3

Problem Orientation: The Intellectual Tasks **34**

Introduction 34
Goals 40
    Shared Power 44
    Participants 44
    Perspectives 45
    Arenas (Situations) 45
    Base Values 45
    Strategies 46
    Outcomes 46
    Effects 48
Trends 48
Conditions 49
Projection 53
Alternatives 55

CHAPTER 4

Diversity: Synthesis of Methods **58**

Introduction 58
Contextual Mapping 63

Developmental Constructs 67
Prototyping Technique 69
Incorporating Computer Simulation 72
Participant Observation and Other Standpoints 74

CHAPTER 5

Professional Services: The Ordinary Policy Process **76**

Introduction 76
The Range of Clients 76
The Problem of Trust 79
The Problem of Complementary Interests 81
The Criteria of Policy 85
  Criteria for the Intelligence Function 86
  Criteria for the Promotional Function 88
  Criteria for the Prescribing Function 90
  Criteria for the Invoking Function 91
  Criteria for Application 92
  Criteria for Termination 92
  Criteria for the Appraisal Function 93
  Criteria for All Functions and Structures 94
Varying Levels of Analysis 95

CHAPTER 6

Professional Services: The Constitutive Policy Process **98**

Introduction 98
The Role of Formulated Authority and Control 98
Goals and Principles 100

CHAPTER 7

Professional Identity **112**

Introduction 112
A Knowledge Network 112
Core Periodicals 114
Encouragement of Continuous General Participation 117
Participation versus Bureaucratism 119
A Distinctive Identity 120
Science, Militancy, and Oligarchy 122
The Inner Structure of Knowledge Institutions 123
Highly Capitalized Science 124
Visibility and Vulnerability 125
Current Proposals 126
Are Scientists Like Everybody Else? 127

Cognitive Maps and Procedures 128
Common versus Special Interests 130
Career Patterns 131

CHAPTER 8

Professional Training **132**

Introduction 132
Context and Specialty 134
Centers, Departments, and Schools 136
Qualifications 137
The Uses of a Prospectus 140
Integration: Study and Field Experience 141
Integration: Problem Orientation 141
Integration: Personal and Situational Contexts 142
The Continuing Decision Seminar as a Technique of Instruction 142
Seminar Requirements and Procedures 144
Seminar Diffusion 155
Supplemental Laboratories 157

Bibliographic Notes **160**

Chapter 1 160
Chapter 2 160
Chapter 3 161
Chapter 4 162
Chapter 5 163
Chapter 6 165
Chapter 7 166
Chapter 8 167

Index 171

Series Editor's Introductory Note

Twenty years ago Harold D. Lasswell, together with Daniel Lerner, introduced the concept "Policy Sciences" and laid down its first foundations, in Daniel Lerner and Harold D. Lasswell, Eds., *The Policy Sciences: Recent Developments in Scope and Method* (Stanford: Stanford University Press, 1951).

Even though the concept was recognized as a revolutionary one and the book itself was widely reviewed and discussed, the idea of policy sciences itself was not followed up until quite recently. Apparently, more progress in various policy sciences disciplines (e.g., decision sciences, applied behavioral sciences, systems analysis), more experience with policy research organizations (e.g., the Rand Corporation and the Hudson Institute) and, in particular, some disenchantment with "normal sciences" and their social consequences, were necessary requisites for accelerated efforts to advance policy sciences. Therefore, it is only now that policy sciences seems to move into its taking-off stage—as evidenced by rapidly increasing interest and efforts in the scientific community and in some groups of policymakers.

The *Policy Sciences Book Series* is directed at serving this interest and supporting the development of policy sciences, by publication of significant texts and studies. No one is better qualified to give us new insight in this area than the originator of the policy sciences idea—Harold D. Lasswell, and, therefore, it is a special privilege to present his book, *Pre-view to Policy Sciences*. This book, indeed, clarifies all aspects of policy sciences, providing a systematic treatment of different issues. For scholars, professionals, practitioners, and students alike, this book constitutes both a thorough introduction to policy sciences and a fundamental work, to be studied and restudied and to accompany the emerging policy scientist throughout his development.

Yehezkel Dror

xi

Preface

In the twenty years since the term "policy sciences" was introduced a remarkable change has come over the orientation of professional training in the realms of culture, biology and the physical sciences. The social sciences have "turned around" far enough to look toward the future. Physicists, biologists and their colleagues are concerned about the social consequencies and policy implications of knowledge. They are reaching across disciplinary lines to consult and work with specialists on government, law and politics. Scientific societies in the United States and elsewhere are appointing committees to consider "science and policy." These committees are beginning to interpret their mandate in much broader terms than the study of sources of money for scientific projects. Transnational conferences are increasing in number and pertinence to problems of public action. New journals and societies reflect the change. Professional schools, academies, and related bodies are undergoing gradual modification.

The trend toward a policy sciences viewpoint—contextual, problem-oriented, multi-method—is a move away from fragmentation. Too often a differentiated approach is permitted to degenerate into a fragmented "worm's eye view" of policy matters. When properly linked with law and jurisprudence, political theory and philosophy, the new instruments of policy analysis and management provide tools of unpreceded versatility and effectiveness. Even an abbreviated list indicates the extraordinary richness of contemporary innovations: operations research, linear and dynamic programming, program budgeting, cost-benefit analysis, systems analysis, forecasting (Delphi and other techniques), computer simulation and gaming, sensitivity training, "brainstorming", decision seminar techniques, social accounting, prototyping.

In developing the policy sciences approach through the years I have had the direct and indirect assistance of associates in many fields. They are literally too numerous to name here. I must, however, make an exception. I have had the good fortune to work closely with Myres S. McDougal at the Yale Law School in evolving a policy sciences approach to law and jurisprudence. One historical figure deserves yet another tribute. The policy sciences are a contemporary adaptation of the general approach to public policy that was recommended by John Dewey and his colleagues in the development of American pragmatism.

On the institution-building front I cannot refrain from referring to the late Beardsley Ruml. Ruml was a prototypical policy scientist. Some of his theoretical writing is directly in point. More notable was his active role as an innovator. For example, Ruml and the late Charles E. Merriam of The University of Chicago were key figures in the interdisciplinary growth of the social sciences (fostered by the formation of The Social Science Research Council). Ruml was a major designer of The Committee for Economic Development (CED), working in close association with Paul Hoffman, William B. Benton, and their associates. When the intellectual and policy history of our time is written, Ruml's contributions will be among the most strategic.

It has been instructive to be associated with, and to observe, both the institution-building and the everyday policy routines of a number of government departments, private foundations, educational institutions, scientific and civic associations, and business organizations in the United States and elsewhere.

The present volume is a short sketch of one of many possible approaches to the policy sciences. The immediate stimulus to prepare this statement came from Dr. Yehezkel Dror, who has already had a major impact on theory and practice in this field.

I am grateful to those who allowed me to draw freely on my published articles, including the publishers and editors of the *Policy Sciences* magazine, the *Journal of Legal Education,* the *American Psychologist,* and *World Politics.* Once more I must acknowledge the generosity of my collaborators, notably Myres S. McDougal, Yale, and Daniel Lerner, M. I. T.

HAROLD D. LASSWELL

CHAPTER 1

The Evolution of the Policy Sciences

A Working Definition

The conception of the policy sciences is more refined and extended today than at any time in the colorful history of man. As a working definition, we say that the policy sciences are concerned with knowledge *of* and *in* the decision processes of the public and civic order.

Knowledge *of* the decision process implies systematic, empirical studies of how policies are made and put into effect. When knowledge is systematic, it goes beyond the aphoristic remarks that are strewn through the "wisdom" literature of the past. The systematic requirement calls for a body of explicitly interconnected propositions such as we have inherited in the Western world from Aristotle, Machiavelli, and their successors.

To insist on the *empirical* criterion is to specify that general assertions are subject to the discipline of careful observation. This is a fundamental distinction between *science* and *nonscience*.

The emphasis on *decision process* underlines the difference between policy sciences and other forms of intellectual activity. By focusing on the making and execution of policy, one identifies a relatively unique frame of reference, and utilizes many traditional contributions to political science, jurisprudence, and related disciplines. However, these *public order* decisions do not exhaust the field of policy. In complex societies the agencies of official decision do not account for many of the most important choices that affect men's lives. In the interest of realism, therefore, it is essential to give full deference to the study of semiofficial and nonofficial processes. The dividing line between *public* and *civic* order is more a zone than a line, and in totalitarian states the civic order is almost entirely swallowed up by public order. The separation is most visible in bodies politic where the activities assigned to the formal agencies of government are relatively few and where the collective activities of businesses, churches, and other active participants in society are independent of detailed direction from government.

The policy sciences find it necessary to keep both public and civic order in view if what is *functionally* important is to be distinguished from merely *conventional* relevance. A commonplace of experience is that the decisions nominally made by governments often register determinations that are made outside government—whether in a bishop's palace, a club of industrialists, or a trades-union headquarters. More generally, in many sectors of human life the norms of conduct are formulated and made effective outside the machinery of legislation, administration, and adjudication.

The reference to *order,* whether public or civic, emphasizes a fundamental feature of the policy science approach. The accent is on *aggregate* problems, causes, and consequences, although a specific problem of a particular organization or individual is not lost sight of. It is fully understood that subtle ties bind every part to the whole. Singularity and typicality are both brought into view when an aggregate is identified.

The policy sciences focus on the relevance of knowledge *in* as well as *of* decision. No one doubts that the realism of a decision depends in part on access to the stock of available knowledge. In our age of science-based technology a task of steadily growing significance is that of anticipating the needs of decisionmakers and of mobilizing knowledge when and where it is useful.

It is, for instance, unthinkable that the Chinese People's Republic could develop a nuclear capability without drawing on the knowledge and skill of nuclear physicists and engineers. Or that the central banks of Western Europe, Britain, and the United States would tackle the problem of monetary stabilization without benefit of economists. Or that the World Health Organization would design a program to eliminate smallpox, cholera, or any other infectious disease without relying on medical scientists. The same point applies to problems that go beyond political security, economic stability, or public health. The problem may be to plan or evaluate programs of mass communication, education, family planning, human rights, the prevention of criminal conduct, or whatever.

Even at this preliminary stage we should comment on the juxtaposition of *policy* and *science* in the term *policy sciences.* The word *science* carries many connotations, one of which is competence in the pursuit of empirically verifiable knowledge. Obviously this connotation is relevant to the task of improving knowledge of and in policy.

In ordinary speech *policy* and *science* carry many less suitable or even unacceptable connotations. Science is often alleged to be value neutral; policy, on the contrary, is commonly assumed to be value oriented. From our point of view it is untenable to assert that scientific activities are value neutral. For scientists, knowledge is itself a valued outcome. No one doubts that the gratification of human curiosity is one of the prime values of man or that scientific inquiry is part of the total process of shaping and sharing enlightenment. In common with all value goals enlightenment may be pursued both as an end in itself (a *scope* value) and as a *base* for the shaping and sharing of other values. Plainly, enlightenment is a goal value for the scientists who are passionately concerned with illuminating the realms of the physical, the biological, and the cultural. And enlightenment is in no sense the only value goal that in various circumstances evokes passionate devotion. No one can live in a new nation that is developing from the status of a colony without recognizing the intensity of the appeal of programs intended to produce individual or national wealth, or power, or health, or skill. In many cases the older priorities of ethics and religion, or even of family affection and loyalty, occupy a lower rank than before.

Part of the connotation of the alleged value neutrality of science is acceptable. Surely the qualified scientist is a participant observer of events who tries to see things as they are. He demands of himself, and of anyone who purports to be a scientist, that he suppresses no relevant fact and that he holds all explanations tentatively, and therefore open to revision if more adequate explanations are proposed. Such is the exploratory, antidogmatic ideal image of the man of knowledge. No matter how utterly sure a scientist may be of the enduring truth of what he has found, the ideal image requires him, when challenged, to reopen his mind to possible change.

The ideal image says nothing about the ordinary passions of man save that anyone worthy of the name of scientist must be able to struggle with considerable success against jealousy, envy, bigotry, and any other attitude that interferes with clarity of perception and judgment. The scientist is not without passion. On the contrary, he utilizes his loves and hates to fuel a motor whose results are subject to the continuing referendum of his peers with regard to empirical validity and formal elegance. No one can read an autobiographical document such as James D. Watson's *The Double Helix* without discovering both the common and the exceptional humanity of the author. The continual spectre that Linus Pauling, the grand old genius of California, would suddenly play a trump and walk away with the pot, leaving Watson and Crick among the "might have beens" of science, did not paralyze; it galvanized. And, in Richard Feynman's phrase, the team had "that frightening and beautiful experience of making a great scientific discovery."

In principle, there are no grounds for believing that the customary criteria included in the ideal image of science cannot be applied by those who study the decision process. It is open to them to describe the flow of events at every level of government and to account for what they see in the light of factors that are also open to reexamination. True, the scientific observer typically needs to train himself to an unusual degree of intellectual detachment from the passions of his contemporaries if he is to make dependable observations and devise unconventional hypotheses for the guidance of inquiry. But this is a difference of degree, not of quality.

The policy scientist does in fact face problems that are present to a less significant degree in ordinary scientific operations. The selection of knowledge for use in decision obviously calls for anticipations of the future. When decisionmakers turn to a given issue, what knowledge will they recognize as pertinent? How much of this pertinent knowledge is presently available, and how can it be assembled and presented by the time it is wanted? Often decisionmakers overlook important bodies of knowledge unless initiatives are taken to change their cognitive maps. How can this be done? As matters stand at present, is important knowledge missing altogether? If so, is there time and are there facilities that might be mobilized to generate the needed knowledge in time? Can decisionmakers be supplied with critical estimates of what is likely to happen (*a*) if they do nothing or (*b*) if they follow a given policy option? Can they be supplied with creative suggestions about the policy alternatives they might adopt?

Without spinning such questions further, it is enough for the present to conclude that the policy sciences must strive for three principal attributes. The first is *contextuality:* decisions are part of a larger social process. The second is *problem orientation:* policy scientists are at home with the intellectual activities involved in clarifying goals, trends, conditions, projection, and alternatives. The third is *diversity:* the methods employed are not limited to a narrow range.

Policy Science Careers

The conception of the policy sciences can be made more concrete by examining the careers of those who are professionally engaged in policy operations. Professional careers in the theoretical branches of policy analysis are no novelty in the United States or in Western Europe, or, for that matter, in any past or present center of urban civilization. Typically these careers are in academic departments and schools where, by tradition, they have had relatively little to do with one another. The reference is to professors of political science, jurisprudence, political economy, public administration, business administration, and so on.

The novelty of recent decades has been the prodigious multiplication of policy science careers in fields having little direct contact with traditional policy theory. The primitive beginnings of such a career may be in a laboratory, a field station, or an archive at a time when the scientist or scholar is absorbed in contributing directly to the advancement of knowledge in his special field. Perhaps he becomes head of a laboratory, a field station, or a library and discovers that he has a gift for mediating between his colleagues and the social environment. The relationship to the environment is twofold: knowledge specialists must be protected; they must receive positive support.

The initial environment may be the modest campus of a college or a university or a public or private research installation. The assets obtained may be equally modest—a few thousand dollars, the political support of an ambitious dean or president, inside knowledge of future plans and possibilities for expansion, the respect of colleagues, the capacity to attract promising theoretical and empirical talent from among those who want to associate themselves with a growing center, and so on. Possibly the mediator is surprised at his own capacity to talk simply and persuasively to colleagues in neighboring fields, and others may take note of the talent.

Hence the next step toward a policy science career may be to move from the care and feeding of a small band of intimate associates to the task of looking after a larger corps of knowledge specialists in relation to a wider social setting. As dean of a school, president of a university, director of a public or private institute or professional society, the individual adapts to an environment whose nonscientific and nonscholarly components are especially important. It is at once apparent, if it were not obvious before, that the social environment is uninterested in knowledge as an end in itself. The inference is that support for the pursuit of knowledge must be obtained by presenting science and scholarship as means, as base values with which to pursue safety and health, wealth, power, prestige, and similar major outcomes.

As the career of a successful intermediary evolves, his perspectives and modes of operation undergo typical transformations. At the beginning he identifies himself with the small group to which he is bound by a common and intensively held subculture of science or scholarship. He perceives himself as a responsible agent, delegate, or spokesman for his immediate colleagues. Hence his specific demands on the social environment are to defend or to improve the group's position. His cognitive map is full of detail about their past, present, and prospective interests. Somewhere along the line the intermediary is likely to undergo a fundamental reorientation. His operations begin to be affected by a map of the social process that is larger than the self-centered extrapolations with which he began. He may make no contribution to the theory of decision, but he is increasingly theoretical in his understanding of what he is doing. A career that began as a purveyor of knowledge for immediate or potential use in policy moves toward the complex role of a full-scale policy scientist who is knowledgeable of the policy process.

Such a reorientation is often accelerated by the opportunities and requirements of government. The go-between who has operated inside the scientific and academic community may be brought into the decision process at any level: municipal, county, state, national, international. A man may begin his career unobtrusively as a technical consultant and pass on to full-time administrative commitments, or occasionally to public leadership.

A transition similar to the change from the academy to government may occur in reference to every sector of society. In the United States it is commonplace to begin a career in the economic process as a business consultant, to advance first to full-time executive and thereafter to an entrepreneurial role as owner-operator of a profit-seeking enterprise. A similar sequence occurs in reference to private health and welfare organizations and so on.

The careers mentioned above may take their origin in any branch of knowledge, whether physical, biological, or cultural. This comes about because collective policies, public or private, may draw upon every scrap of kowledge anywhere in the vast storage system of society. We have been indicating how the knowledge specialists themselves take initiatives to obtain support from the social environment. They call attention to the utility of specific forms of knowledge in contributing to the realization of the value goals of more and more participants in the national, transnational, or subnational community.

Note that as yet we have not mentioned a set of developments whose impact on the policy processes of society has been peculiarly important. I refer to knowledge innovations that have influenced policy in a far more fundamental manner than by providing information pertinent to a particular policy issue. Procedures have been changed. These procedure-innovating operations are reflected in the spectacular expansion of the electronics data storage and retrieval industries, the explosive growth of management consultative services, and the proliferation of training and other professional institutions in policy fields.

The careers of those who specialize in some aspect of "knowledge *of* policy" develop in much the same way as the careers of the specialists who belong to the "knowledge *in* policy" category. One group, for instance, is interested in a specific computer model, and may or may not provide the enlightenment or skill required to gear it effectively into the policy process of a customer or client. Another advocates or sells a specific cost-benefit-risk system; another emphasizes particular simulation procedures; another stresses a survey technique for obtaining estimates of the future; another promotes free-association techniques of creativity (e.g., "brainstorming"); and so on. In a competitive world—whether of profit or nonprofit operations—those who devise specific techniques are likely to adapt to the prevalent selling patterns of the society, and to leave problems of integration—if they think of them at all—to the invisible hand celebrated by Adam Smith.

Stemming from the fantastic creativity, threat, and opportunity of our time is a growing current of interest in cultivating a sounder knowledge of the invisible hand, even where there is no disposition to usurp its function. Looking back at their experience, many policy science operators wonder whether they could save others from the mistake of arousing unfulfillable expectations—hence of giving the newer procedures a black eye—or from the mistake of disregarding destructive side effects on the policy process or on the biological and physical environment.

The sequences outlined above are similar in the United States, in Great Britain, and in countries where the role of government, though of enormous importance, is less conspicuous than in Socialist or Communist polities. In the latter the established ideology emphasizes the interdependence of society and environment and prescribes a vanguard role for the political order and the agencies of government. The policy science approach, which elsewhere is left to pluralist competitors or functional oligarchies, is, with reservations, the official doctrine of the established order.

The reservations in these circumstances are not trivial. Although the contextual character of the policy science approach is insisted upon, it is in fact circumscribed by adherence to orthodox views of the past and future. Hence it is not permissible for private or official persons to reject the image of a future that includes the inevitable triumph of the particular institutions endorsed by top decisionmakers in the name of the established ideology. This includes optimism about the results attainable when resource allocation and utilization are centrally directed, and belief in the ultimate erosion of coercion to a level that constitutes a free man's commonwealth.

Policy scientists in Great Britain, the United States, and other countries with a relatively effective tradition of free speech are also subject to career restrictions if they explicitly reject the orthodox view of the virtues of privately owned and operated business modified by government regulation and enterprise. Although such careers are restricted, it is nevertheless true that the pluralistic and spatial diversity of the national context is such that it is possible to build a tolerated career in unorthodox circles.

In nations where the private control of resources is a principal feature and where military-police methods are employed to prevent sweeping alterations of structure, policy scientists are circumscribed by the controlling oligarchy, which means that deference must be given to doctrines compatible with the outlook of the colonels, the landlords, the tribal elders, the foreign investors, or the foreign official or unofficial allies.

Where policy scientists are comparatively free to define their role, a significant convergence of view can be demonstrated among them. We note that policy approaches tend toward *contextuality* in place of *fragmentation* and toward *problem-oriented* not *problem-blind* perspectives.

If the starting point of a given specialist has been one of the disciplines historically identified with knowledge of decision, the tendency has been to amplify each discipline until it can be expressly related to its neighbors. This is a reversal of nineteenth- and early twentieth-century trends toward specialization, when political philosophy, for example became a relatively remote scholarly domain where logical exercises dominated the subject. More recently the tendency has been to search for contact with the rich flow of human experience and with the evaluation processes inherent in every institution.

If the specialty of origin of a policy science career was academic political science, the concern for the explanatory or scientific mode of thought has been supplemented to include policy-oriented concern for the attainment of such fundamental goals as effective democracy or efficiency without bureaucracy.

If the special field of origin of the policy scientist was constitutional or international law, the tendency has been to focus on the attainment of an authoritative and controlling public order, where war would be obsolete as a strategy of collective action.

If the starting point was economics, the main stream has been to recover and expand the conception of a truly comprehensive political economy preoccupied with the development of modernizing economies or with the stable growth of relatively developed economies.

Similarly, the practitioners of every other branch of the cultural arts and sciencies and of biology and the physical sciences seek to clarify and realize the social consequences and policy implications of knowledge.

We referred before to procedural innovations that have become the specialized interest of a subprofessional group concerned with decision. Some members of the new skill groups are finding it important to perceive their role in a wider setting. Therefore they tend to pass from extreme specialization on management technique toward a policy science generalization. At the same time the traditional theorists of decision, concerned with the mastery of theory and empirical detail, are moving not only toward one another, but toward the specialists who introduced the new technologies.

The result is that policy science careers are not only contextual and problem oriented; they include a distinctive synthesis of techniques of every kind, whether they involve the gathering or processing of data, or the formation of theories or solutions.

Historical Trends

The significance of contemporary developments is illuminated when we take a long view of the past. We do not approach the past in a nostalgic frame of mind, nor do we limit the study of history to the modest task of answering specific questions that are topical at the moment. We believe that if the past is approached contextually, it is possible to achieve novel perspectives on the configuration of all events—past, present, and future.

Suppose we ask under what circumstances the policy sciences begin to appear. When do the decisionmakers and the thinkers about decision achieve a level of self-awareness that enables them to evolve a systematic view of the process?

Evidently the critical point is an evolving self-awareness; and this was probably connected with the relatively sudden emergence of civilization from the largely anonymous sea of tribal or folk societies. The first civilizations sprang rather suddenly into view about the fourth millennium B.C. in the river valleys of the Nile, the Tigris-Euphrates, and the Indus. Every sector of soceity was affected: in terms of *wealth,* the new urban division of labor greatly enhanced productivity and widened the gap between rich and poor; as to *enlightenment,* the advent of literacy provided the means of storing and retrieving information on an unprecedented scale; in regard to *respect,* social classes were highly differentiated along occupational and income lines; in matters of *rectitude,* such as religion and ethics, the local gods were subordinated to the high gods of the rulers, and in the long run secular norms gained impact; in the sphere of *affection,* kinship and extended family units were weakened by individual mobility and the territorial state; in reference to *skill,* the expansion of education gave rise to new intellectual specialists whose decisive role is only now becoming obvious; in all that touches on *well-being,* such as safety, health, and comfort, civilization implied almost incredible extremes; in the realm of *power,* urban civilization marked the emergence of institutions such as the territorial state, formal legislative codes of law, regular taxes, bureaucratized civil and military operations, monumental public works, complex systems of taxation, and official records.

It is true that the great systematizing treatises on public decision do not date from the earliest civilizations. We are accustomed in this connection to think of Aristotle and Plato in fifth century Athens (500 B.C.) and of Confucius or Kautilya in China or India. These treatises are unimpeachable evidence of systematic thought about public order and processes of decision. There is little doubt, however, that a relatively systematic view of man, nature, and society was taken by those who prepared the early codes of law, such as Ur-Nammu of Ur (of the twenty-first century B.C.) and Hammurabi (the sixth king of the Amorite dynasty of Babylon, the eighteenth century B.C.).

Codifiers faced the formidable task of bringing together in one authoritative instrument a synthesis of traditional and novel elements. For the first time in human history, writing was available as a means of stabilizing the expectations of the community about authoritative norms and sanctions. Contrary to a view that is believed to have prevailed in tribal societies, where legislative innovation was not frankly accepted, the authorities in the city-states and empires could no longer tolerate many traditional arrangements appropriate to a tribe or a narrower kinship group. A new social situation generated a new focus of attention; a new focus of attention generated new experience, including self-awareness. In turn, new demands and expectations arose, in which older ways of doing things could be thought about and deliberately continued, modified, discontinued, and superceded. Codifiers deliberately altered the allocation and exercise of public authority and control, and adapted many prescriptions to fit the perceived advantages of the ascendant elite.

Although most of the earlier codes survive as fragments, it is clear that they were not haphazardly organized. They were often formulated with great clarity and simplicity, and they contained few enigmatic components. Hammurabi's code no longer recognized such tribal practices as blood feud, private retribution, or marriage by capture. The punitive sanctions were adapted to the requirements of urban society and imply that thought had been given to the behavioral consequences of threatened deprivations of varying magnitude. Rights and obligations were graduated according to status, and many measures were taken for the express purpose of protecting the poor against exploitation by public officials and others.

While it was customary to exalt rulers, there are indications that some of them were indeed wise and vigorous men. It is evident that the structure of urban society made it possible for educated classes to participate in public affairs and to engage in administration, adjudication, negotiation, teaching, and many other differentiated activities. The emerging class of educated men were the "symbol specialists" of society. We are particularly interested in those members of the class who achieved a relatively comprehensive view of public policy, and who made use of their knowledge for policy purposes.

Symbol specialists did not appear for the first time in human history with the emergence of true urban societies and the invention of writing. In tribal cultures some specialists executed the brilliant murals in the caves of southern France, northern Spain, and many sites in Africa and elsewhere. In many, if not in all, tribes there were magicians or medicine men who excelled in the performance of ritual acts.

In both tribal and urban society a distinction is to be made between two categories of symbol specialists. Some magicians or medicine men served individual clients, who solicited their services for such particular purposes as guaranteeing fertility or obtaining success in the chase. Some specialists, on the other hand, were expected to explain, prophesy, or influence collective outcomes, such as the harvest, a plague, or a war party.

Every ritual operation calls for at least some degree of specialized knowledge. The degree may be very modest indeed, as when a routine prayer (or prayer equivalent) is uttered for the health of a person who makes a standard gift in payment. All the operator needs to know is how to utter the words and to execute the ritual gestures involved. In marked contrast, however, are ceremonies that are recognized to concern the safety of the entire tribe. Typically such rituals are guided by an elaborate body of knowledge that refers to the past, present, and future of the tribe. For instance, if planting ceremonies are held at the wrong time, they may be perceived as losing their potency. Therefore, the symbol manipulator must possess a comprehensive cognitive map that enables him to choose the season of the year and to judge the most propitious alignment of sun, moon, and stars. The date may be connected with the supposed origins and movements of the tribe, so that the appropriate members of the community are deployed in a formation expressing continuity and solidarity.

The relevant distinction is one between symbol specialists who combine skill with enlightenment and those who use skill with little or no enlightenment.

Enlightenment implies a relatively comprehensive map, and the ritualists who serve the whole community are expected to understand such a map. Presumably this depends on training and on possessing attributes that render a person eligible in the first place to obtain such training. Although it is not universally true that essential knowledge is narrowly held by a few, one usually finds that the elders as a group, or particular elders, are perceived by themselves and others as having more inclusive and dependable knowledge than individuals who are chosen at random. In many cases a lifetime is none too long to obtain mastery of the esoteric knowledge indispensable to the role.

In contemporary terms those who combine skill with enlightenment are *professionals,* while those who are in command of a specific skill are members of an *occupational* or hobby group. Because knowledge has depended to such an extent on written modes of communication, we are accustomed to think of professionals as members of a learned group who have familiarized themselves with an appropriate library. As skills grow complex, the book shelves for an occupation also lengthen. However, despite the tendency to converge, the basic distinction remains valid. The true professional can manipulate an armory of skills with awareness of *aggregate* consequences in mind. This, we note again, was the significance of the magician for the tribe and for the individual. Likewise, the priest-theologian of the early cities was undoubtedly perceived as a professional, since he was presumably in a better position than others to know the cosmic plan.

The emerging policy scientist in our civilization is not only a professional in the sense that he combines skill with enlightened concern for the aggregate processes and consequences of decision. He belongs among the systematic contextualists who are also empirical. It is the steady rise of the empirical, or scientific, component that separates the fully developed policy scientist from the appliers of dogmatic theology or metaphysics.

Without pretending to isolate unvarying sequences, it is possible to identify several long-range, empirically significant trends which have been conditioned by the cumulative growth of civilizations and whose relationship to the policy sciences is apparent. We can follow the rise of astronomy from astrology; of chemistry and physics from alchemy; of physicians from medicine men; and of the social, behavioral, and policy sciences from early practitioners of witchcraft, divination, and sorcery. Empirical methods improve; transempirical perspectives grow dim. The movement has been from the fear and propitiation of nature, or of individual and collective personifications, to universal religions and secular ideologies. Some secular myths appeal to faith in history or science as sources of absolute knowledge of coming events. The empirical techniques and the tentative perspectives of science are of relatively recent prominence or weight; they are incompatible with claims for absolute knowledge of the future, even in the name of science, since they put the accent on probability, not inevitability.

When we summarize the contemporary expansion of the policy sciences in the long perspective of the past, we see a change that is deeply embedded in the expansion and differentiation of urban civilization in world history. We provisionally define the policy sciences as concerned with knowledge *of* and *in* the decision process. As a professional man, the policy scientist is concerned with mastering the skills appropriate to enlightened decision in the context of public and civic order. As a professional man who shares the scientist's disciplined concern for the empirical, he is searching for an optimum synthesis of the diverse skills that contribute to a dependable theory and practice of problem solving in the public interest.

CHAPTER 2

Contextuality: Mapping the Social and Decision Processes

Introduction

Contextuality is an unescapable theme for the policy scientist. To be professionally concerned with public policy is to be preoccupied with the aggregate, and to search for ways of discovering and clarifying the past, present, and future repercussions of collective action (or inaction) for the human condition. In a world of science-based technology every group and individual is interdependent with every other participant, and the degree of interdependence fluctuates through time at the national, transnational, and subnational level.

As living forms, *human beings interact by taking one another into account*. Whether we speak of the problems connected with the control of nuclear energy for peaceful purposes, the voluntary or compulsory control of population, the prevention of plague, the spread of knowledge and education, the encouragement of the expressive arts, the protection of human rights, the protection of the natural environment from wasteful use, or any other major issue, we come rapidly to the conclusion that the world is not only interdependent, but that realistic and selective awareness of that interdependence is indispensable to enlightened public policy.

To assert that a professional man, such as a policy scientist, is distinctively concerned with the *aggregate* is not to imply that he can serve only the government. In many societies only a few decisions are left to official institutions. This does not, of course, signify that all nongovernmental decisions are insignificant for the aggregate. The historian and analyst of bodies politic where the government did little may demonstrate that the decision-makers in the economic, ecclesiastical, familial, and other sectors did well or badly; but at least they had a profound influence on the health, wealth, education, political unity, or crime level of the entire society. In such contexts part of the role of the policy scientist is to assist all decisionmakers—official or nonofficial—to take aggregate consequences into account.

If the policy scientist is to think contextually, how is this to be done?

Clearly, we need guidance on *what* to think about or look for, and on *how* to proceed. The first requirement calls for principles of *content* (or manifest meaning); the second, for principles of *procedure*. Both guidelines are needed by *an individual who is acting for himself* and by *individuals who are playing either an official or a nonofficial role*.

In the first chapter the policy scientist was classified among professional men of enlightenment and skill, and his frame of reference and competence were described as including the decision processes of both the public and civic order. Hence principles of content are needed to provide a guide to locating the policy scientist and his clients in the knowledge process and in all other sectors of society. A suitable map must find a place for client relationships (with students, colleagues, and sustainers of research, and with official and nonofficial individuals and organizations). In some circumstances the policy scientist is his own client in the sense that he clarifies his preferred goals on controversial issues in the decision process and acts accordingly (by running for office, engaging in active promotion, etc.). He may identify himself with a professional association of policy scientists and act to influence and give effect to association policy in the wider context. Certainly a comprehensive cognitive map is an indispensable tool in aid of self-orientation *toward* clients and in providing orientation *for* clients. Principles of procedure will be discussed after the content of an inclusive contextual map is given consideration.

A Social Process Model

We have underlined the point that the context in which and with which the policy scientist interacts is the social process, and that in a world of science-based technology the social process context is, in principle, the globe. Hence the most generalized image of the whole must be formulated in such a way that it can be applied to the world community, or to any territorial or pluralistic context within the larger configuration.

The simplest representation of a social process emphasizes the participants (the actors), the flow of interaction (the interacts), and the resource environment:

Actor ↔ Actor

Actor ↔ Resource environment

Since the actors are living forms, they participate selectively in what they do. We describe this selective characteristic by the *maximization postulate,* which holds that living forms are predisposed to complete acts in ways that are perceived to leave the actor better off than if he had completed them differently.

The postulate draws attention to the actor's own perception of alternative act completions open to him in a given situation. If he perceives himself as hungry, the tendency is to perceive the environment (social and physical) in terms of food and to reach for objects that have been satisfactory in the past. It is convenient to think of an act whose locus is the individual as a sequence of events beginning in impulse and passing through a phase of subjectivity to expression.

Impulse   →   Subjectivity   →   Expression

(including perception) (including behavior)

The sequence does not imply that perceptions are irredeemably tied to specific internal events (such as hunger or lust). At any given moment it is probable that many impulses are activated in some degree. Hence the precipitating event may be incoming messages that testify to the immediate availability of objects that seem better adapted to the gratification of one rather than another impulse.

Further, it is not implied that a perception is necessarily valid: It will not inevitably be corroborated in subsequent experience. For instance, the liquid perceived as wine may turn out to be hair tonic.

Nor is there an implication that a perceptual event is always slow and deliberate. It may be instantaneous and unconscious.

Perceptions are not invariably conditioned by the same proportion of *acquired* to *inherited* components. Some reflexes, such as grasping, are preorganized in the genetic code. Other responses, such as spoken language, are heavily modified by past conditioning and selective learning during infancy and childhood.

The maximization postulate refers to act completions that are perceived by the actor as leaving him better off than he would otherwise be. What criteria are employed in these perceptions of relative advantage? Some criteria are preorganized in the genetic code and occur in sequence when a given state has been reached. The act that includes searching for food (which includes sucking and swallowing) is organized to include perceptions of being gratified. However, these components are loosely organized in the infant and are patterned in detail on the basis of experience with the environment (nursing, etc.).

Hence from the earliest hours the human infant is interacting with others. These interactions are the components of the social process that provide the most diverse features of the process. In brief—

Interaction

Actor A acts ↔ Actor B acts

The diagram leaves open to intensive study the discovery of who initiates which act and of how the act completions of A and B are affected at each phase. What does the scientific observer of the *interact* choose to classify as a culminating event in the sequence?

When he first examines a social process the observer is impressed by the "seamless web" of life. None the less, some "seams" must be found if differentiation is to be possible. The most direct device is to select *culminating outcomes,* that is, events that are generally understood in a given situation to be very desirable (or undesirable) happenings.

Preoutcomes   →   Outcomes   →   Postoutcomes

The culminating events in a given culture are not very difficult to identify. In decision processes, for example, one is usually able to recognize such outcomes as the settlement of a dispute or the holding of an election. In more intimate matters, an outcome such as marriage or the breakup of a marriage are conspicuous. These occasions are perceived by the participants in the common culture as of great importance for the positive or negative gratification of the participants. They can indeed be viewed as outcomes to which more or less prolonged preoutcome interactions led and from which subsequent consequences flow.

Social scientists have often ignored the distinctive nature of their fundamental frame of reference and attempted to impose classificatory systems extrapolated from other fields, notably the biology of simpler organisms. Inventories have been made of specific reflexes exhibited in the infant, and subsequent responses classified in ways that made it convenient to recognize, for instance, a sucking or swallowing component. But such a criterion (convenience in identifying such partial components) is secondary to the concern of the social analyst. His most distinctive frame of reference is furnished by the context of culture, particularly the practices characteristic of adults. The prehistory of an adult pattern in the life of any individual is a history of gratifications (positive or negative) in preadult culture. To explore these sequences is a complex task that is not necessarily lightened by reflex inventories.

The model utilized here proposes categories of reference to the shaping and sharing of outcomes (values) by employing practices (institutions) that in the context are relatively specialized to each value. The revised social process model reads as follows:

Participants → seeking to maximize values (gratifying outcomes) →
utilize institutions → affecting resources

(The arrows may also run the opposite way in order to emphasize interaction.)

If a short list of value categories is employed by the analyst, it is manageable. And if the list can be readily applied to all societies, contemporary or historical, it is well adapted to the requirements of science and policy.

The following model uses eight value terms to classify the nearly infinite number of preferred outcomes:

Value	*Example*
Power	Victory or defeat in fights or elections
Enlightenment	Scientific discovery, news
Wealth	Income, ownership transfer
Well-being	Medical care, protection
Skill	Instruction, demonstration of proficiency
Affection	Expression of intimacy, friendship, loyalty
Respect	Honor, discriminatory exclusion
Rectitude	Acceptance in religions or ethical association

It may be clarifying to spell out the point that these outcome events, in common with all events in a social process, are interactions. (See table 1.) To receive power is to be supported by others; to give power is to support others. To receive enlightenment is to obtain knowledge of the social and natural context; to give enlightenment is to make such knowledge available

TABLE 1

Social Process: General

For convenience the social process can be broadly characterized as follows:

    Participants→seek values

        →through institutions

        →affecting environment

The process is outlined, with more detail, in the following table:

Participants	Perspectives	Situations	Base Values	Strategies	Outcomes	Effects
Individuals	Value demands	Unorganized	Positive assets	Coercive	Value	Values
Groups	Expectations	territorial	perspectives	Persuasive	indulgences	accumulation
Value shapers	Identities	pluralistic	capabilities	assembling,	deprivations	enjoyment
official	Myths	Organized	Negative assets	processing	Decisions	distribution
nonofficial	doctrines	territorial	perspectives	(polarity:	Choices	Institutions
Value sharers	formulas	pluralistic	capabilities	multi-,	intelligence	structure
official	mirandas		(power, enlighten-	pluri-,	promotion	function
nonofficial			ment, wealth,	tri, bi-,	prescription	innovation
			well-being, skill,	uni-)	invocation	diffusion
			affection, respect,		application	restriction
			rectitude)		termination	
					appraisal	

to others. To obtain wealth is to receive money or other claims to the use of resources for production or consumption; to give wealth is to transfer money or claims. To receive well-being benefits is to obtain the assistance of those who affect safety, health, and comfort; to contribute to well-being is to assist others in the same way. To obtain skills is to be provided with opportunity to receive instruction and to exercise an acquired proficiency; to contribute to the skill of others is to enable them to have corresponding opportunities. To receive affection is to be an object of love, friendly feeling, and loyalty; to give affection is to project these sentiments toward others. To receive respect is to obtain recognition from others; to give respect is to grant recognition to other people. To receive favorable evaluations in terms of rectitude is to be characterized as an ethical or religious person; to evaluate others in terms of rectitude is to characterize them correspondingly.

Receiving and giving may be further supplemented or complicated by refusing or withholding. In any case an interaction can be summed up as *value indulgent* or *value deprivational* for the participants. To be indulged is to occupy an improved position in the social process; to be deprived is to occupy a worsened position.

A common example of value indulgence at the level of world politics is obtaining access to a national market, or defeating initiatives to exclude the nationals of a nation state from the market. Value deprivation, on the other hand, occurs when previous access is prohibited, or access is blocked in the first place. In general—

$$\text{Value indulgence} = \text{Gain, blocked loss}$$
$$\text{Value deprivation} = \text{Loss, blocked gain}$$

From the standpoint of a particular participant in a social process, or of the participants as a whole, the interactions can be summarized in terms of value shaping and sharing, and especially of value priority, accumulation, distribution, investment, and enjoyment.

An important step in analyzing these dimensions of the social process during any time period is to sum up gross and net outcomes.

$$\text{Gross value outcome} = \text{Value indulgences received}$$
$$\text{Net value outcome} = \text{Gross outcome less value deprivations}$$

We are most accustomed to make these distinctions in terms of wealth production and to subtract costs from income. But the corresponding categories also apply to the shaping (production) of all values. For instance, a nation state may enhance its power by being named to the Security Council of the United Nations. However, the direct and opportunity costs in terms of power may be commitments that limit freedom of choice on issues that come before the Council. A scientist may contribute to the advancement of knowledge in the field of weapon development, but his costs may include foregoing a contribution to knowledge in nonweapon areas. The cultivation of well-being by programs that reduce the incidence of one disease includes the cost of progress that might have been made in conquering another. The acquisition of high levels of skill in sport may have involved the sacrifice of skill in the arts. The choice of one set of friends may be incompatible with the friendship of others. Similarly the respect obtained from persons outside one's social caste or class may cost the respect of persons of one's own class. The contribution that one offers to public morality by refusing to make an unworthy appointment may entail as a cost the moral denunciations uttered by adherents of a different code of rectitude.

For many scientific and policy purposes the position of individuals and groups can be described according to their share in the values shaped during a given period. In large-scale societies we are accustomed to assume that values are unequally distributed, and to refer to elite, mid-elite, and rank and file according to the degree of control over values. Income figures amply bear out the expectation of inequality, and although the correspondence is far from perfect, it is not far wide of the mark to assert that in most modern states inequalities of economic income are roughly paralleled by inequalities of power, well-being, and all the other values.

Information about current levels of value shaping and sharing makes it, in principle, possible to calculate gross and net changes in aggregate or particular value status.

Net value change = Values at the beginning of a period plus or minus net value outcome at the end of the period

In the disposition of values a distinction is drawn between investment and enjoyment. When a value is invested, it is employed in the shaping of further values of the same kind; when a value is enjoyed, it is used to obtain other values. A common example is wealth investment, as when plant and equipment are expanded. Enjoyment (consumption) entails the use of income for values other than wealth, such as recreation (well-being), education (skill), party contributions (power), mass media and scientific publications (enlightenment), family amenities (affection), sociable clubs (respect), and church contributions (rectitude).

A parallel analysis is applicable to values other than wealth. For instance, power can be invested in pursuit of more power, as when votes on issues are traded for votes for a higher office. Power may be enjoyed as a base for obtaining respect (as by exploiting the ceremonial possibilities of an office), enlightenment (as in the case of inside information), wealth (as when a boss receives stocks and bonds in return for influence), or other values.

For some purposes it is helpful to subdivide further the *enjoyment* of a value, and to separate its use in shaping another value from its use in sharing the value. We mentioned the enjoyment of power when it was employed to obtain wealth, and this is separable into gaining control over instruments of production (wealth shaping) and products for final consumption (wealth sharing). In regard to respect, for instance, power may be enjoyed as a means to gaining admission to an upper-class social club, which is a permanent improvement of status, or it may be used for a ceremonial dinner, which is a once-and-for-all affair.

At this point it may be helpful to clarify the distinctions between *values* and *institutions*. We defined values by calling attention to culminating events. Institutions, we specified, are the patterns that are relatively specialized to the shaping and sharing of a principal category of values.

Value	*Institution*
Power	Government, law, political parties
Enlightenment	Languages, mass media, scientific establishments
Wealth	Farms, factories, banks
Well-being	Hospitals, recreational facilities
Skill	Vocational, professional, art schools
Affection	Families, friendship circles
Respect	Social classes and castes
Rectitude	Ethical and religious associations

Institutions refer to the same events that are designated by the *value* terms; they make it possible to formulate fundamental questions about the interplay between any specific institution and the value-shaping and value-sharing processes which the institution affects, and which it in turn affects. Contextual analysis implies that every institution influences and is in turn influenced by every institution specialized to its value sector, and potentially by every institution in every other sector. However, the inference is that mutual impacts are variable through time; hence, the effects occurring at one period are not necessarily the same as the results at earlier or later times. Furthermore, it is implied that the effects attributable to one institutional practice in one situation are not necessarily distinctive. Hence, it is a mistake to prejudge empirical inquiry and to entertain dogmatic convictions that a specific institutional pattern necessarily produces similar results, or is always conditioned by the same constellation of factors.

This contextual, inquiring point of view treats all the self-serving declarations current in the world with reserve. Assertions about the "inevitable" consequences of a specific institutional practice or system of practices are neither accepted nor rejected out of hand. They are turned into hypotheses for empirical evaluation. The challenge is to explore and to keep up-to-date in the appraisal of how, for example, self-described democracies work. (Self-description is part of the perspectives of an institution.) Are these self-declared systems "democratic" when they are assessed in reference to the actual flow of decision? Is it possible to appraise the impact of the governmental system on enlightenment, wealth, and all the other sectors of society? The contextual approach calls for the examination of all the "justifications" put forward by the ideologies of "democracy," "absolutism," "science," "socialist methods of production and distribution," "freedom from anxiety," "the arts," "love," "freedom from discrimination," "religious faith," or whatever.

Thus far the exposition has been kept in relatively abstract terms. The allusions made in the preceding paragraph remind us that, however abstract such categories may be, they are of a level of generality that occurs in the decision processes of the globe at many levels. Latent in the conceptual system of all known political, economic, and religious institutions are categories of equal or greater abstraction. If we are to communicate as policy scientists in the decision arenas of the United Nations, or of any less inclusive context, it must be possible to operate smoothly with (and on) such abstractions.

However, it is not implied that as policy scientists we dwell exclusively at the level of high abstractness. As empirically oriented professionals it is our responsibility to connect general categories of reference to the policy process, and to the place of anyone in it, including ourselves, by means of appropriate procedures. The principles of procedure by which general terms are systematically related to one another and to actual situations are part of the equipment essential to a policy scientist. He is distinguishable from the layman by his hard-won competence in subjecting doctrinal generalities of all kinds to the sobering process by which empirical meanings, if any, are ascertained. As a mediator-integrator among many men of knowledge and action, the policy scientist is a necessary specialist on empirical validity.

Hence the social process model must be open to whatever degree of specification is deemed pertinent in a given context. The elaboration of the model brings out the following:

Participants →
　Perspectives →
　　Situations →
　　　Base values →
　　　　Strategies →
　　　　　Outcomes →
　　　　　　Effects →

The *participants* are all who interact in a social context chosen for policy analysis:

Individuals
Groups
　Unorganized
　Organized
Value shapers and sharers

Every individual or group participant is to some extent a value shaper and sharer in every value-institution sector of the social process. The shapers of power include the active political leaders and officials who also share power. The producers of wealth share the benefits according to the pattern of distribution. The same point applies to those who take the lead in formulating criteria of excellence (skill), distinction (respect), or morality (rectitude). They also share the opportunity to acquire and exercise skill, to receive recognition, or to be favorably assessed in ethical terms.

The *perspectives* are the subjective events experienced by the participants in the social process.

Perspectives	Myth
Identity	Doctrine
Demand	Formula
Expectation	Miranda

Perspectives of identity include the *I, me,* or the *primary ego symbols.* The primary ego symbols are joined with symbols of reference to other egos to constitute a *self* ("we Americans," "we policy scientists," etc.). Some ego symbols of reference are excluded from the self to comprise a *not-self other* ("those Canadians," "those industrialists," etc.).

The perspectives of demand are preferences and volitions. They are value demands and can be conveniently classified according to the eight categories of the model. Value demands are "by the self" and may be "on the self" or "other than the self." Further, the self as a whole or any component identity makes value demands. In my role as a politician who is identified with the destinies of a political party I join in demanding increased power for the party and increased values of all kinds (such as money for campaigns, and endorsement by famous figures [respect] and by churchmen [rectitude]).

Perspectives also include expectations, which are the matter-of-fact references to past, present, or future events. Included are causal assumptions as well as particular allusions. Sanguine expectations present the future as value indulgent; pessimistic expectations, as value deprivational.

Myth is a term of art designed to refer to all relatively stable and coherent patterns of perspective. (The implication is not that these perspectives are necessarily true or false in the empirical sense.) Every individual or group develops a distinctive myth, for which terms like ideology, counterideology, and the like are available. The *doctrinal* components of a myth include the more abstract statements (the philosophy). By the *formula* is meant the prescriptive norms of conduct that are adhered to on pain of deprivational sanction. The *miranda* are the relatively concrete and expressive elements, such as the popular culture.

The *situations* referred to in the model are the zones in which interactions occur.

Situations = Ecological or spatial dimensions
Temporal dimensions
Unorganized, organized
Value inclusive or exclusive
Crisis or intercrisis

We recognize that the globe as a whole is a situation, since the degree of interaction is high enough to affect what goes on. The time period with which we are concerned may be prolonged (as the duration of urban civilization) or brief. Situations may be inclusive of significant components of all values (as the nation state) or they may be specialized to a particular value or sub-value (as in the case of a pluralistic association). The crisis level may be high (as in war) or low.

The *base values* include all the values available to a participant at a given time. It is clear that a political party, for example, has some political power, thanks to the public officials and bosses under its control; possesses enlightenment assets if it has access to radio, television, and printed media; enjoys wealth to the extent that money and volunteer services are available; marshals physical vitality in the degree that it draws on youth; attracts love and loyalty from those who are identified with its past and future; draws respect from various social strata; and commands a reputation for moral integrity from the record of its leaders.

Strategies are the management of base values to affect value outcomes. In terms of elementary components an act is composed of the following:

Symbols = Events of reference (subjective events)
Signs = Resources specialized to mediating between the perspectives of communicators (sounds, print, etc)
Nonsign operations = Body movements of a nonsign character (walking, etc.)
Nonsign resources = Resources of body (the soma) and physical features of the environment (the objects produced in manufacturing, etc.)

Some strategies are relatively specialized to the use of signs (communication) or other resource elements (collaboration):

Communicative strategies
    Diplomacy = messages among elites
    Propaganda = messages including nonelites
Collaborative strategies
    Military = Resources used as weapons
    Economic = Resources used for nonweapon purposes

Many other categories are helpful in distinguishing strategies from one another. Without going into detail we mention only *persuasive and coercive* instruments and strategies that mix value indulgences and deprivations in different combinations, and that join the values in distinctive patterns.

We have dealt briefly with value outcomes and effects above.

A Decision Process Model

Since the policy scientist is particularly concerned with the power process, he must operate with a contextual map that gives special prominence and refinement to outcomes—initially in the power sector and later in all the sectors.

The categories of *perspective* and *operation* provide convenient tools for identifying, with more precision than before, the distinguishing characteristics of power outcomes. Such culminating events are relatively important (1) in terms of the values at stake and (2) in terms of the unforceability of the commitments made by the use of severe sanctions against possible challengers. These dimensions must be estimated according to expectations and realizations, which requires that perspectives must be confirmed by operational reality.

These criteria are stated in functional, not conventional, definitions and require empirical knowledge before they can be applied to any concrete situation. Ordinarily we expect to find that the conventionally recognized institutions of government, law, and politics include a large part of the important decisions in a given community. But investigation will probably disclose that by no means all of the statutes passed by a legislative body, for instance, are expected to be enforcible against possible challengers by the use of severe deprivations (such as capital punishment, confiscation of property, or heavy fines). Investigation may also show that the values affected by many statutes are perceived as relatively inconsequential. Hence in the functional sense the votes that passed the original statutes were not power decisions.

The policy scientist is often able to make a significant contribution to the assessment of governmental institutions by stressing the degree of difference between the conventional language of a body politic and the facts of power. It is also possible to clarify the conception of lawful power, and to facilitate the understanding and use of legal instruments.

Consider, for instance, the relationship between power as control and power as authority:

Power
    Lawful = Controlling and authoritative
    Naked = Controlling, not authoritative
    Pretended = Authoritative, not controlling*

* *Naked* power and *pretended* power are *incomplete* power; *no power* (or *nominal power*) is *no authority, no control*.

Authoritative expectations include assumptions about who (selected how and exercising his control how) will be generally regarded as justified in what he does. In passing, it may be noted that authority may be recognized, even though not approved. It is, however, an unstable situation if a potentially strong minority regards established authority as unethical, irreligious, or otherwise deficient. Any authoritative expectation exerts *some* control. The political situation is unstable when a potentially strong minority looks upon the established order as unethical, irreligious, or in other ways reprehensible.

The distinction between severe and mild sanction and the magnitude of the values at stake clarifies the meaning of public order and civic order. Public order includes all the institutions of power and the fundamental features of every value-institution process: they are protected by the flow of authoritative and controlling decision at the outcome phase of the political process. In some societies every interaction that occurs anywhere in the social process is guided in detail by political decisions. Such a society is *politicized;* it is often called *totalitarian,* or a "garrison-prison state," as a means of stressing the degree to which coercive outcomes have absorbed the whole social process. *Liberal* societies give a more modest role to government; and *anarchical* theorists advocate a coercionless world as a utopian goal ("a free man's commonwealth").

The fact that the distinctive reference frame of the policy scientist is the decision outcome does not imply that he may not specialize on problems that occur at a particular phase of the total policy act of a body politic. On the contrary, his conceptual map must provide a guide to obtaining a realistic image of the major phases of any collective act. For this purpose we embellish the social process map with a more detailed presentation of decision as a sequence of seven phases.

Our model of the decision process distinguishes seven power outcomes:

Intelligence →
  Promotion →
    Prescription →
      Invocation →
        Application →
          Termination →
            Appraisal →

The *intelligence* outcome includes the gathering, processing, and dissemination of information for the use of all who participate in the decision process. Among the specialized official structures are overt and covert intelligence agencies (e.g., census, CIA), forecasting services, planning organizations, and censorship bureaus. It is obvious that in totalitarian powers coercive strategies are extensively employed to keep the flow of intelligence in the approved narrow channels. But coercion is universally used for many intelligence operations, such as the use of subpoena power to compel testimony or the employment of negative sanctions to prevent the circulation of forecasts in advance of public announcements. In open societies coercion is chiefly employed as a means of protecting competitive access to information sources and channels.

Promotional outcomes add agitational intensity to the dissemination of a value demand. A regular feature of totalitarian regimes in modern times is the monopolization of promotional activities. Typically promotion is in the hands of a single political party (more accurately called a "political order") whose largely ceremonial activities are protected by the police. The organization of new political parties is forbidden in fact, if not in form, although a few "micro-parties" may be tolerated for purposes of foreign propaganda.

Prescription outcomes are characterized by the stabilization of expectations concerning the norms to be severely sanctioned if challenged in various contingencies. The structures specialized to this function include constitutional conventions, legislatures and assemblies, and executive authorities that promulgate regulations.

Invocation is the act of characterizing a concrete situation in terms of its conformity or nonconformity to prescription. The police, grand juries, and lower courts are highly specialized to this role. So, too, are all the administrative agencies that begin to operate in specific situations in accord with regulations.

Application is the final characterization of concrete circumstances in terms of prescriptions. This is the distinct task of appellate courts, for instance, and of most of the bureaucratic structures engaged in public administration.

Termination cancels a prescription and deals with the claims put forward by those who acted in good faith when the prescriptions were in effect, and who stand to suffer value deprivation when they are ended. In societies where innovation is rapid, new structures are often needed to cope with claims of the expropriated for compensation or relocation, for instance.

The *appraisal* outcomes characterize the aggregate flow of decision according to the policy objectives of the body politic, and identify those who are causally or formally responsible for successes or failures. Legislative or executive commissions are authorized to conduct investigations and to come up with appraisals of the kind. In totalitarian powers any organized initiative of this kind is strictly repressed.

The examples given above are chosen from the internal arena of a nation state or subnational unit. They are equally relevant to less highly organized decision processes, such as the arena of intergovernmental and international relations. The prescriptions of international law, for instance, may depend on the standard expectations current among the foreign offices of nation states as these are reflected in bilateral negotiation, as well as in decisions of international courts.

The examples above were also limited for the most part to governments, although mention was made of the role that may be played, and defended as part of the public order, by nongovernmental structures such as the free press and a competitive political party system.

As a means of relating this model more explicitly to conventional structures of the public order, it will be useful to amplify the analysis of power arenas (situations) in the social process schematization. The categories are restricted to organized and specialized structures of varying degrees of inclusiveness.

Inclusive and comprehensive (world community)

World government (hypothetical): Aggregate of
Intergovernmental, multipurpose (e.g., United Nations)
Intergovernmental, particular purpose (e.g., World Health Organization)
Transnational, multipurpose (e.g., transnational political parties)
Transnational, particular purpose (e.g., transnational pressure groups)
Transnational, occasional purpose (e.g., other transnational organizations)
Transnational, varying domain (e.g., individuals operating transnationally)

World Polarity
Unipolar (authoritative and controlling; hypothetical)
Bipolar (two superpowers; U.S.A. and USSR after 1945)
Tripolar (three superpowers; hypothetical addition of China, Japan, or unified Western Europe)
Quadripolar (four superpowers; hypothetical addition of two)
Pluripolar (a few major powers)

Polypolar (several major powers)
Multipolar (many approximately equal powers)

Centralization-decentralization (in single territorial or pluralistic organizations)
Number of vertical levels (e.g., nation-wide; states, provinces, or regions; urban; county, township; ward; block or cell)
Number of units at each level (by membership or spatial size)
Inclusive authority and control of aggregate at each level (including multi-purpose or particular purpose organizations)
Exclusive authority and control of each unit at each level (included in each aggregate organization)

Concentration-deconcentration (in single territorial or pluralistic organizations)
Number of horizontal units (sharers of authority and control at each vertical level; e.g., in the United States at the most inclusive level, the Presidency, Congress, Supreme Court, civilian military departments; the electorate, political parties, pressure groups, other private organizations and individuals)
Exclusive authority and control of each unit (Inclusive authority and control is identical with the level of centralization above, save when two or more subunits are organizing to constitute a new unit to share their previously exclusive power.)

The decision map can be most readily understood if we relate it to some political terms in current use. No one of these words carries altogether satisfactory connotations to the specialized policy scientist. He will, nevertheless, often find it expedient to employ these words as a means of effective communication. Moreover, connotations provide a stimulating point of departure for inquiries that may uncover matters of general interest.

For example, nation states and systems of public order may be called—

Unitary
Federal
Confederate

Unitary states are usually thought of as territorially contiguous entities (like France) which are formally independent of the external authority of any entity of the same kind. If the entire globe were an inclusive and comprehensive authoritative and controlling body politic, its decision structure would be unitary. A *federal* structure is also a territorial entity that enjoys the same status in the world arena as a unitary state. But territorial units are conceived as having important power over some important policy tasks (as in the United States, where the states are alleged to possess reserve powers). When the scope of common action among territorial entities is narrow, it is usual to refer to *confederations, leagues,* or *permanent alliances.*

Interstate systems historically and currently follow complex organizational channels:

Diplomatic
Parliamentary diplomatic

Some distinctions emphasize the organs that are supposed to interconnect the top executive with the electorate.

Parliamentary: Top executive committee, legislature, electorate
Presidential: Top executive, legislature, electorate
Soviet: Top executive committee, council, assembly, electorate

Although authority is exercised in the name of all members of the body politic, the members of a general electorate are alleged to give ultimate expression to fundamental policy goals. The top executive may be one or more officials formally selected by the electorate or by intermediate organs. A legislative body meets frequently and plays an active role in the total policy process. Assemblies, on the other hand, meet infrequently and, despite their high authority, are commonly controlled from the center. Executive councils are more continuously active and may intermittently dominate the top executive committees. The top committee may or may not be controlled in fact, though not in terms of formal authority, by a single person. The distinction between formal authority and effective control is particularly obvious when a ceremonial top executive (whether a president or a monarch) exists alongside an effective executor, such as a prime minister.

Some terms emphasize permanent administrative entities:

Bureaucracy: Territorial
Bureaucracy: Corporative

In the Roman Catholic Church the hierarchy of officials has been largely self-perpetuating (papacy, cardinals, bishops, etc.) and selected "from the top down." In theory the corporative form of organization could emphasize pluralistic associations who diversify tasks at horizontal levels and modify the vertical departmental system.

Finally, a vast number of terms emphasize the supposed degree of authority or control actually exercised by individuals and small groups in the body politic, acting at all phases of decision.

Monocracy:　The one
Polyarchy:　The few
Democracy:　The many

No matter how highly differentiated a map of the social process may become, the initial model (man seeking to optimize value outcomes through institutions affecting resources) is a fundamental frame of reference for the policy scientist. It enables him to distinguish the power-institution sector from other sectors of society, and to identify the several outcomes in the decision process. Such a functional device enables the user to describe the role of *conventional* structures and functions in any situation relevant to his purposes.

How does the policy scientist relate himself to the problems that arise in contemplating or manipulating any particular context, inclusive or limited? These are the next questions to which we turn.

CHAPTER 3

Problem Orientation: The Intellectual Tasks

Introduction

The life of a decisionmaker is a life of commitment. It is a life of saying yes or no, or of avoiding direct answers. The career is full of opportunities to discover problems that have previously been beyond the attention of those who might do something to hasten their resolution. The greatest contribution of an active politician may be to arouse the community to recognize danger, whether from within or without, and to mobilize the intense and continuing demand required to search for and put into effect the policies that defend or fulfill the value goals of public and civic order.

A commonplace of experience is that the leading figures in the decision processes of a modern body politic are under enormous pressure. Legislators may be expected to make up their minds and vote on hundreds, even thousands, of proposals that get as far as a draft resolution, committee deliberation, or floor debate. The president, governor, mayor, or other chief executive is under more unrelenting pressure than anyone else, since it is assumed that he has the heaviest impact on decision.

The principal actors are subject to the constraint of time. If a chief executive devotes much time to a single issue, other problems suffer relative neglect. The cost of absorption in foreign affairs is typically paid in the domestic arena and the other way round.

The man who tries to keep on top of his responsibilities is likely to suffer from chronic fatigue and exasperation, and unless he has an exceptional natural constitution, a quick mind, and selective habits of work, he falls farther and farther behind. The more he knows about the full scope of his potential influence, the more bitterly the conscientious man feels about the physical and psychological limitations that constrict his performance. He perceives that his impact falls far short of either need or opportunity. In a man of conscience the private tensions mount as the discrepancy grows. For some they are too heavy to bear. This is the private history of some surprising acts of self-destruction among prominent leaders. It explains the occasional crack-up that uses mental illness or psychosomatic disorder as a means of escape from what has become a hell of gilded futility. The appraisal of the "self by self" is fantastically different from the appraisal of the self by loving friends, admiring constituents, and frustrated opponents.

Most conscientious men of the power elite are able to carry the load by mitigating the severity of the sentences that they pass privately on themselves. They perceive the danger of perfectionism, sensing that if they demand too much they will end by doing too little. Suicide or moods of torpid melancholy, or seizures by obscure somatic troubles, destroy potential service to cherished goals.

Men of conscience and power who master their internal tensions with insight are fortunate. More commonly, tensions are dealt with by devices other than insight and understanding. Defense mechanisms take over. Self-critical moods and images are swept aside. Tendencies to feel "anti-self by self" are reacted against by the technique of substitution. Instead of feeling powerless, stupid, improverished, depressed, unlovable, clumsy, shameful, or guilty, one permits the opposite feelings to take root. One allows one's self to feel powerful, brilliant, rich, euphoric, lovable, superskilled, proud, and righteous.

As a rule, however, substitutive mechanisms do not work perfectly. If they did, a leader might succeed in becoming tolerable to himself by becoming utterly intolerable to others; and community self-defense may eventually put him in a psychiatric hospital or a prison, or retire him from public life in less emphatic fashion. Since internal mechanisms do not usually operate with total success, some measure of outside support is sought. We find that men of power typically evolve a subculture of mutual reassurance and support. The operational rules of the game call for enormous doses of reciprocal respect. Everyone is inundated in a warm bath of complementary adjectives, adverbs, and significant gestures. There are elaborate expressions of love and affection. A "club" atmosphere keeps public exchange of vituperative remarks to a minimum and paves the way for private rituals of symbolic reconciliation and restitution. There are convivial occasions of private relaxation, and these range over all the outlets offered by the culture.

The public style of the active political man is dictated in detail by the images and acceptances built into his social environment. Americans and Western Europeans have evolved a "paranoid" style, in which grandiose demands are made on immediate, intermediate, and public circles. In other societies the principal figures cultivate a "benign" style.

In some societies the culture is so unreservedly committed to the exercise of power that inner restraints are at a minimum, and ambivalent attitudes do not occur. The arch type is the chief of a nomadic tribe, who finds it easy to engage in the herding or killing of people. The desert conqueror and his tough, rough cohorts project a vivid and terrifying image to the agriculturalists, tradesmen, artisans, and officials of settled river valleys and coastline communities. The classical literature of China, for instance, faithfully reflects the apprehensions generated by the threats from inner Asia. On a more modest scale the mountaineer plays a role comparable to the desert nomad. And there are brigands of the sea, who, in Viking style, operate from island or peninsular bases, from which they plunder the inhabitants of less militant localities.

The imperial subjugators and colonizers who exploited the emerging technology and urban assets of Western Europe, and spread into the Americas, mid-Africa, Asia, and Africa in the imperialist period were men of militant action. Lurking on the scene, though not yet able to make themselves effective, were the politicians of mass revolt, who played a progressive role in changing the structure of power from within the nation states of Europe, and initiated a succession of ideological and organizational waves that transformed, however incompletely, the public order of Europe and eventually of the Europe-affected domain.

In the large-scale nation state and metropolitan world of today the universalizing culture of science-based technology has challenged traditional value priorities and institutional forms. The inner and outer pressures on all who engage in processes of decision are multiplying.

Nevertheless, the picture we have painted of the harassed and fatigued decisionmaker is a partial exaggeration, in its implication that all decisive acts occur under the gun of instant and overwhelming necessity. A power figure who experiences life in these terms is a man who allows himself to exaggerate the immediate. Contrary to the stereotype, it is quite feasible to find time in a life of active decision for continued and intensive examination of a selected set of problems. The image of the overpressured official, when true in fact, is a confession of weakness by an undisciplined person. Of course it also serves as a convenient alibi for warding off inconvenient demands.

Anyone who survives for a few years in public life is quite likely to develop areas of specialized knowledge and competence as a result of his exposure to particular areas of public policy. If he is a legislator, areas of growing expertise may be connected with committee assignments or with the network of interests on which reelection depends. Perhaps the politician has succeeded in diverting attention from his involvement with the copper, coal, cotton, or other commodity interests in his constituency by becoming an articulator and clarifier of the common interest in areas that touch him less closely. For instance, he may exercise a mighty influence on behalf of human rights or peace or governmental reorganization.

Whatever the modern decisionmaker's mode of adjusting to outer and inner pressures, he turns with more frequency than before to scientific assistance in attempting to cope with his problems. He is accepting the fact of contextuality and adapting himself to two implications. First, every problem of policy has ramifications that require expert attention. Second, specialized assistance is useful in mobilizing needed knowledge and judgment.

Awareness of complexity and *acceptance of specialized assistance* vary from place to place, and from one function to another. At the national level the problems of security and modernization have brought more knowledge into decisionmaking and execution. At the subnational level the plight of the cities has proved "too important to leave to the politicians." Or, to phrase the point with more accuracy, the values at stake are too important to entrust the future of the community to obsolete conceptions and procedures of public problem solving.

The first recognition of complexity coupled with the demand for expertise was made by the executive agencies of government. Executive agencies face realities that go beyond arranging words in formal documents. They must make immediate changes in overt acts (deeds) and physical resources. In a world of science-based technology the output of words cannot be allowed to reach such inflated levels that deeds are not affected and resource changes do not occur. Deflationary effects are equally dangerous. We are well aware of the fact that when money and credit are insufficient, downward cycles of buying, investment, and production may continue until structural damage is done to the economy. Similarly, when the words employed in executive orders and directives are few or cryptic or irrelevant, the acts necessary to maintain public order may not be performed. Putting out fires, purifying water, or disposing of garbage calls for verbal directives that are realistically related to physical as well as conventional realities. Under these constraints executive agencies have been learning to reconsider their problem-solving methods in the light of available knowledge.

The legislative branches of government have been relatively slow to recognize or adapt to new complexities. They have been held back by the nature of the activity in which legislators are most highly specialized—the production and exchange of words. Deeds and things may be obscured by verbal smog. Symbolic inflation is a chronic state, since in the legislative arena words generate words. More specifically, words of complaint and condemnation elicit answering complaints and condemnations. These negative references—these expressions of deprivation—also invite symbolic reassurance.

Strictly speaking, the problem of the legislator is not words in general, but the misuse of words. *Symbol inflation,* not *symbol use,* is the problem. The balance between relevant and irrelevant words is upset in the direction of irrelevances. Symbolic adjustment calls for a middle range between inflationary and deflationary expression. To inflate is to indulge in dramatization, fantasy, and deception; to deflate is to ignore or mislead by neglecting to mobilize attention and support on behalf of needed action.

More legislators are perceiving that the fate of legislatures as institutions of public order depends on improving the realism of their symbolic output. This, in turn, depends on the mobilization of knowledge. Unless legislatures succeed in achieving a contextual and problem-solving level of functioning, they will not long endure. Where the executive branch does not already control, it will take over, partly from superior realism, partly from tactical superiority in the management of coercion.

Even a cursory projection of the future requires us to go beyond the official organs of government. A common error in public policy analysis is to give insufficient attention to the semiofficial or private components of the total process, especially in the conduct of promotional activities. At first glance the hundreds and thousands of political parties and pressure organizations seem more tied to the expediencies of the moment than do the legislatures. Such an impression soon calls for drastic revision. The key policymakers in many of these associations are committed to long-range objectives. They are well aware of the importance, in redesigning institutions, of going beyond estimates of immediate support to consider how future operations may succeed in generating the perspectives and the coalitions necessary to survival and to realize the objectives sought. Problem-solving activities are not necessarily limited to a few hours, days, or months. They may involve long time intervals. Long periods of planning, promotion, and appraisal may be preconditions of effective changes in the prescribing, terminating, invoking, and applying functions of government. Much of the work must be done by private organizations—political parties, pressure groups, or other private associations. Recognition of the importance for public policy of knowledge and specialization has been spreading among the private groups who expect to maintain their identity over long periods, and who perceive that they will benefit if their own policy processes take long-range objectives and strategies adequately into account.

A contextual map, we have said, is an indispensable preliminary to the examination of any particular problem. The map does not, however, supply the answers. It provides a guide to the explorations that are necessary if specific issues are to be creatively dealt with.

An adequate strategy of problem solving encompasses five intellectual tasks. Five terms carry the appropriate connotations or can acquire them readily: goal, trend, condition, projection, alternative. (Many equivalent analyses are in current use; as usual, the important point is not choice of term but equivalency of concept.)

Goal clarification: What future states are to be realized as far as possible in the social process?

Trend description: To what extent have past and recent events approximated the preferred terminal states? What discrepancies are there? How great are they?

Analysis of conditions: What factors have conditioned the direction and magnitude of the trends described?

Projection of developments: If current policies are continued, what is the probable future of goal realizations or discrepancies?

Invention, evaluation, and selection of alternatives: What intermediate objectives and strategies will optimalize the realization of preferred goals?

The categories imply principles of *content* and *procedure.* As guides to content, they are reminders of questions worth raising in the consideration of any problem. As procedural principles, they imply the wisdom of performing the various tasks in an orderly manner. Since apart from its context no detail can be adequately understood, the five questions furnish an agenda for allowing the context to emerge at the focus of individual or group attention. For example, a fundamental principle is that postulated goals are to be held *tentatively* until they have been disciplined by exposure to the consideration of trends, conditions, projections, and alternatives. The most productive procedure is to examine the whole problem by returning again and again to the separate tasks.

The social and decision process map must be clarified and kept relevant to the five tasks. Preference maps must be critically compared with one another as a means of clarifying value goals. Trend maps are essential to summarizing the historical sequences that realize or fail to realize preferred goals. Scientific maps are needed in order to bring together available knowledge of which conditioning factors have had which trend consequences.

Relevance also calls for maps that project future developments in the degree to which preferred events are approximated or fail of approximation. Finally, maps are required to invent specific policy objectives that are compatible with overriding goals, and to weigh comparative value benefits, costs, and risks.

We have referred to the policy scientist as a professional man who is qualified to increase the visibility of relevant events. To stress aggregate effects is not to imply that the policy scientist is unable to serve individual clients. The economist or the lawyer who advises a private corporation, for example, does not reduce his helpfulness to the corporation by recognizing the aggregate processes that affect his client, or that will in turn be affected by his client's corporate policies. The inference is that *parallel acts* may be as significant for aggregate consequences as *explicitly collective acts*.

The line of demarcation between the involvement of the whole community and of specific individuals is not always clear. Even in tribal societies the distinction was far from simple. A chief might consult a medicine man to improve the health of the tribe by getting rid of the plague. Or he might focus on his personal problem and seek to improve the health of his son and heir presumptive. In form the latter request does not relate to the value position of the whole society. If, however, the tribe is strongly identified with the chief and his son, the public order is partially at stake. Sometimes individual clients may receive the same interpretation of their difficulties from a single source, as when a magician suggests that their troubles are attributable to the declining potency of the chief. Each consultation may be private. However, the parallel impact constitutes a collective act whose effect may be to alter the position of the chief and of all who are closely connected with him.

If the policy scientist is to play his clarifying role in collective or private circumstances, we assert that he must fully understand his own position. To some extent we are all blind and no doubt will remain so. But there are degrees of impairment, and so far as decision outcomes are concerned, it is the responsibility of the policy scientist to assist in the reduction of impairment.

Goals

The goal-clarifying task is indicated by the blunt question, "What ought I to prefer?" An individual may refuse to ask such a question of himself. But *no* answer means acceptance of past answers, and the continuation of unconscious or marginally conscious adherence to them. The only options open to the individual or the group are either to think about an issue or to conform to past residues of thought and near-thought. Even the act of thinking about the justification for nonthought is to reject the omnipotence of nonthought.

Inclusive preference models answer such questions as these: What priorities do I prefer in the shaping and sharing of values in the social process? What levels of value accumulation and what pattern of sharing do I prefer?

The great theological and metaphysical systems of mankind offer comprehensive doctrinal answers to these questions, and it is apparent from human history that attempts to interpret and apply these doctrines have influenced the evolution of values and institutions. When examined analytically, each doctrine can be shown to contain two classes of statements with a policy science reference. One class formulates *norms of conduct*. The other states the *transempirical propositions* in terms of which the norms are justified. The transempirical propositions are theological or metaphysical. They may assert, for example, that the realization of human dignity in human affairs is consistent with the will of God (or of many gods) or that it is consistent with impersonal forces in the universe.

In his role as scientist a policy scientist does not perceive himself as qualified to pass judgment on the validity of competing claims of a transempirical character. His competence is restricted to the confirmation (or disconfirmation) of statements about the perspectives or the operational events in social process. His religious or metaphysical convictions need not interfere with his integrity as a scientist if he does not assume that the empirical truth of a proposition is increased by emphatic affirmations that it is so.

If the policy scientist is precluded in his professional capacity from arbitrating among the conflicting assertions of theology and metaphysics, is he precluded from identifying himself with value goals? Definitely not. On the contrary, we interpret problem orientation as requiring him to clarify his goal preferences, since he is bound in some measure to affect value realizations. We propose that his professional concern with adding to the visibility of these consequences be applied to himself (and the profession).

How does the policy scientist set about his goal clarifying task? An initial step is *to search for postulates of sufficient generality to provide guidance in coping with the problems that arise in connection with the shaping and sharing of values.*

A fundamental issue is whether the overriding aim of policy should be the realization of the human dignity of the many, or the dignity of the few (and the indignity of the many). If the goal is the former, decision outcomes should aim at achieving equal opportunity for participation in power, wealth, well-being, and all other valued outcomes. The implication is that basic institutions ought to be open to continuing appraisal in order to ascertain their contribution to realizing and maintaining a social process in which human dignity is optimally realized. In contrast, the goal of dignity for the few, rather than the many, calls for the permanent ascendancy of *some* men. Among the more conspicuous ideologists of this kind have been the apologists for imperialisms of religion, class, or race.

Having formulated high-level generalizations about preferred goal, what next step is open to the policy scientist? *General statements must be specified in sufficient detail to enable them to be considered contextually.*

A suggestive aid in moving from high-level abstraction toward specification is afforded by the Universal Declaration of Human Rights, which outlines some of the implications of human dignity. (The task of specifying a human "indignity" model can be executed by generalizing, for instance, the Nazi program for non-Aryans.)

1. *Well-being.* The Declaration recognizes the right to "life, liberty and security of person" and condemns "torture" as well as "cruel" or "inhuman" treatment or punishment. There is a "right to rest and leisure" and a general right to "social security."

2. *Affection.* The Declaration specifies the "right to marry and to found a family" and to engage in congenial association with others ("peaceful assembly and association"). And there is the right to be identified with a national community ("right to a nationality").

3. *Respect.* The first article affirms that "all human beings are born free and equal in dignity and right. . . . Everyone is entitled to all rights and freedoms . . . without distinction of any kind." Obviously, there must be no "slavery or servitude," no arbitrary interference with "privacy, family, home or correspondence," and freedom from attacks on "honor and reputation."

4. *Power.* The Declaration asserts the right "to take part in the government," "to be recognized as a person before the law," and "to effective remedy by competent national tribunals." Criteria of fair trial are enumerated together with a right of asylum. There is a right to "a social and international order."

5. *Wealth.* Recognition is given to the "right to own property" and to a "standard of living adequate for the well-being" of the individual and his family.

6. *Enlightenment.* There is "freedom of opinion and expression" and a right "to seek, receive, and impart information and ideas through any media and regardless of frontiers."

7. *Skill*. Recognized is the "right to work, to free choice of employment," and "to protection against unemployment." Also "everyone has a right to education" and "to participate freely in the cultural life of the community, to enjoy the arts and to share in scientific achievement and its benefits."

8. *Rectitude* affirms "freedom of thought, conscience and religion. . . . Everyone has duties to the community," and there is no right to destroy the freedom of others.

The policy scientist cannot be satisfied with a goal commitment until it is tested by all the techniques at his disposal. What happens to his preferences if he takes himself as an object of inquiry and considers the factors in the past that have predisposed him to make this commitment? To what extent have these orientations been conditioned by his past environment? (Obviously these are the *trend* and *condition* questions in the problem series.)

To discover that acceptance or rejection of human dignity can be predicted from past exposure to culture, class, interest, or personality environments does not imply that the commitment should or should not be continued in the future. The point of self-examination is to loosen the bonds of automatic affirmation. It is also pertinent to reevaluate the costs and consequences that follow the realization of high or low levels of human dignity.

An important implication is that even if individuals and groups adopt the policy sciences approach they may continue to differ on fundamental goals. Policy sciences with conflicting value postulates can, and presumably will, exist. There can be policy sciences of human dignity and of human indignity in the same way that there are biological professions specialized to life (medicine) and to death (biological warfare).

Questions of professional practice in relation to a client will be considered later in the context of related issues (chapter 5).

We recognize that exercises in systematic goal clarification are most likely to occur during the early stages of professional training. However, it is not necessarily true that serious and repeated efforts at goal clarification are utterly impracticable in later life. Think of the number of people who include in their annual calendar a few days of participation in retreats under the auspices of religious or secular associations. Or take note of the circulation of books and periodicals that deal with religious and ethical questions. Or add the number of persons who listen to sermons or attend lectures on theological or philosophical issues. No matter how strident and ephemeral the content of the daily media, millions of human beings continue to engage in private meditation and prayer, or turn for long-range spiritual and moral assistance to clergy, psychiatrists, and other professional or nonprofessional sources.

These allusions are intended to challenge any tendency to dismiss as entirely impractical the suggestion that disciplined examination of value goals is feasible. (It should go without saying that we are not suggesting that all traditional procedures are well adapted to today's requirements.)

A relatively systematic formulation of the value goals of human dignity must specify the principal components of each value (participants, perspectives, situations, base values, strategies, outcomes, effects). Because of our concern for the shaping and sharing of power, we provide some indication of what is involved.

Shared Power

Controlling and authoritative power is shared to the extent that the following requirements are fulfilled:

Participants

1.0 The political myth favors the pattern of general participation in decisionmaking.

1.1 Communications are in harmony with this perspective and include the prevailing doctrine, formula, and miranda (popular lore).

It is affirmed that people are the ultimate source of authority and endorse procedures by which the popular will can be expressed. The people may act directly on questions of policy or choose officials whom they hold responsible.

1.2 Participation in decisionmaking is, in fact, general.

This proposition refers to deeds. Overt participation occurs when most, if not all, mature people are sufficiently interested in community questions to take part in their solution. Hence voting frequencies are high.

It is evident that perspectives are inferences from two sets of data, one summarizing communications, the other, acts of collaboration. As indicated above, data of both kinds are required before a scientific observer can make a final judgment of the distribution of perspectives that conform to the myth (or the intensity of these subjectivities). Experience shows that the pictures obtained by analyzing words and deeds separately do not jibe with one another. Thus the percentage of qualified voters who go to the polls may be high, though confidential interviews may show great scepticism about the fact that the will of the people is effective. Our goal model specifies a situation in which confidence is widespread that general participation is efficacious—and confidence is supported by corroborating experiences. Experience acquaints us with situations in which high frequencies of voting by

qualified persons may occur only occasionally. Nevertheless, confidential interviews may indicate that popular will is believed to be truly effective
whenever the voters bestir themselves. In the goal situation we are content
with only moderately high frequencies if all the indicators of popular control, considered as a whole, indicate genuine sharing.

Perspectives

These are most directly covered in each entry of the present outline, where
the initial entries refer to myth (and its doctrine, formula, and miranda) or
to the component symbols of identity, value demand, and expectation.

Arenas (Situations)

2.0 The political myth favors organized and unorganized arenas in which
power is widely participated in, and perspectives and capabilities are sustained that are compatible with the sharing of power.

2.1 Expressed preferences are for:

2.11 *Organized* arenas over *unorganized* arenas when unorganized arenas undermine, or are in danger of undermining, shared power.

2.12 *Public order* arenas over *civic order* situations only when coercion
cannot be avoided and must therefore be monopolized by the body politic.

2.13 *Constitutive* arenas adjusted to inclusive and exclusive power interests.

These interests depend on the relative degree of involvement, high or low,
in power interactions. The adjustment of interests guides the arrangement of
detailed arena patterns to obtain optimized advantage, bending the balance
now in one direction, now in another, as the evaluation suggests. For example, governmentalized-private, territorialized-pluralized, centralized-decen-
tralized, concentrated-deconcentrated, regimented-individualized, durable-
temporary.

2.14 *Other than constitutive public order* arenas adjusted to inclusive
and exclusive interests, according to relatively high or low involvement in
power as it interacts with other values. The optimum arrangement of detailed patterns is adjusted according to inclusive and exclusive interests.

2.2 Overt operations (deeds) harmonize with expressed preferences.

Base Values

3.0 The political myth favors access to base values affecting power according to individual merit as a human being and as a contributor to common interests.

3.1 Expressed preferences are for:

3.11 The allocation of fundamental equality of power to every individual.

Fundamental equality is necessary to maintain personal integrity and the integrity of the system as a whole.

3.12 The allocation of other values to the extent they are minimally essential to sustain the fundamental level of individual power.

3.13 The allocation to individuals and structures of the power required to serve the common interest (and the withholding of more power than is essential to the task).

This is a precaution against the generation of special interests as a result of excess power. It carries with it precautionary presumptions against more power, whether inclusive or exclusive, than is required by the common interest, especially in reference to arena structure. Hence presumptions are against excess power in any direction (as enumerated in 2.13).

3.2 Overt allocations harmonize with expressed preferences.

Strategies

4.0 The political myth favors the use of noncoercive operations to influence decision. Noncoercive operations must be employed with sufficient frequency and intensity to sustain high levels of predisposition in the body politic to participate actively in power processes.

4.1 Expressed preferences are for:

4.11 The use of noncoercive strategies.

4.12 The mobilization of sufficiently universal coalitions to sustain high levels of involvement with political participation.

4.2 Overt activities are compatible with expressed preferences.

Outcomes

5.0 The political myth favors decision outcomes that use minimum coercion, maintain the fundamental value-institution patterns of public order, and achieve decisions that optimize preferred values.

5.1 Expressed preferences are for:

5.11 Outcome practices that must rarely depend on coercion to sustain the common interest.

5.12 Outcome practices that accord with, and continually reaffirm in action, the fundamental features of the public order system.

5.13 Outcome practices whose decisions contribute to the optimizing of preferred values.

5.14 Outcome practices that carry out each phase in harmony with basic objectives:

5.141 An intelligence outcome that clarifies objectives, describes trends, analyzes conditions, projects developments, and formulates policy alternatives.

5.142 A promotional outcome that mobilizes attention to and demand for possible policies of common interest.

5.143 A prescriptive outcome that crystallizes general expectations in regard to a set of public interest norms, contingencies, and sanctions:

5.1431 Prescriptions distinguish goal and instrumental norms from one another.

5.1432 Contingency statements in prescriptions are sufficiently definite in terms of content and procedure to permit the relevant situations to be identified.

5.1433 Sanctions in prescriptions are adapted to the following objectives:

5.14331 Deterrence of acts of deviation.

5.14332 Restoration of the situation prior to deviation.

5.14333 Rehabilitation of the value deprivations occurring during periods of deviation.

5.14334 Prevention of deviation by diminishing provocations and by increasing positive indulgences, while remaining within the system of public order.

5.14335 Correction of deviational individuals who are incapable or unwilling, despite standard educational opportunities, to conform to the requirements of public order.

5.14336 Reconstruction of public order, which will be unnecessary when the model is attained (save possibly when new forms of life or extraterrestrial communities are encountered).

5.144 An invoking outcome that gives prompt provisional effect to prescriptions in concrete situations.

5.145 An applying outcome that gives adequate final effect to prescriptions in concrete circumstances.

5.146 A terminating outcome that puts an end to prescriptions that are relatively noncontributory to the common interest, and disposes, in ways most advantageous to the common interest, of claims that have crystallized during the period in which the prescription was authoritative and controlling.

5.147 An appraising outcome that summarizes the degree to which the policies of the public order system are achieved in fact, and the appropriate assignment of responsibility.

5.2 Overt operations harmonize with expressed preferences.

Effects

No distinctive specifications are required for postoutcome events. They are included in the overriding perspectives and are realized as the social process unfolds. (A parallel analysis is ultimately called for in reference to the other seven values of the social process model, which in addition to power includes enlightenment, wealth, well-being, skill, affection, respect, and rectitude.)

Trends

The nature and relevance of trend thinking has been indicated in the earlier discussion of how comprehensive goals can be clarified. The most direct result of trend description is to show which participants in the social process have fallen short of such goals as those specified in the Universal Declaration of Human Rights and elaborated above. We give more detailed consideration to the technicalities of trend analysis when we analyze appraisal outcomes in later chapters. The immediate aim is to suggest that much can be accomplished in a problem-solving strategy that gives full weight to asking and answering the questions, "Where are we? How far have we come in achieving what are aiming at? Where are the positive and negative instances of success or failure?"

The search for contemporary and historical indicators of the degree to which human dignity is realized may reorient the traditional preoccupation of historians. On the whole, the historians of Western Europe and the United States have been neglectful of the lower strata of society. As might be expected a scholar conforms to the maximization postulate in choosing his topic and utilizing his methods. Why study a problem for which the documentation is notoriously unsatisfactory? The kings and presidents of the world go to great pains to influence subsequent history by providing at least partially accurate archives. The poor do not. If we ask how the lower classes perceived themselves and others, and whether they kept alive a strong undercurrent of partly conscious protest against inequality, we are rarely able to find an answer. On the other hand, we are impressed by the clues that the historian is able to recognize when he applies himself to the task. Once scholars have accepted the legitimacy of such a problem they show great diligence in searching for remnants of popular culture that were formerly discarded.

The term *trend* has one connotation that must be set straight. We do not limit our interest to continuous sequences that lead from yesterday to today. It is relevant to locate events of any period that are similar to current happenings or which reveal sharply contrasting episodes, situations, and epochs. In their search for similarities in a mass of seeming dissimilarities, historians have been guided by many theoretical conceptions. The most grandiose of these retrospective conceptions tells us that history has always moved in cycles. If we set aside for the moment any critical evaluation of the claim of cyclical theories to scientific status, the immediate point is that the cyclical conceptions inspire attempts to locate our epoch at some stage in the current cycle. In view of our concern for human dignity the question arises whether recurring movements toward or away from equality are demonstrable. In this connection it will be recalled that Aristotle utilized the rich history of the Greek city-states to indicate the ephemeral though allegedly recurring character of government by the masses, as indeed of any form of goverment. Under the influence of unilinear versions of evolution the march of history has sometimes been interpreted as a one-way path toward "the free man's commonwealth" (allowing for detours).

In addition to goal clarification, trend thinking is affected by every other intellectual task in the problem-solving repertory. The analysis of conditions, for example, will probably draw attention to features of the past that are otherwise de-emphasized or overlooked in the quest for indicators of goal realization. These features are the constellation of variables that can be cited to explain the direction and magnitude of past achievement. When we consider projections into the future, attention may be given to developments that have been little examined by past historians, and which stimulate renewed interest in past situations. For example, the invention, evaluation, and tentative selection of policy alternatives may point to the importance of "passive" or "internalized" periods in the past.

Conditions

The intellectual task called the analysis of conditions is the scientific pattern of thought. A scientific orientation does not allow us to take cyclical theories seriously unless it can be shown how they are generated by the changing strength of interacting factors in a theoretical model of the social process. A

challenge inherent in the third problem-solving task is to identify the factors
that affect the realization of human dignity and, if possible, to discover their
routines of interdependence.

The mode of thought that provides a guide for scientific inquiry often utilizes an equilibrium model. According to this conception, a pattern of relations can be identified that, when disturbed by outside factors, tends to be
restored. Thus if one scans the events of the past two hundred years in
France, it is possible to select years in which power has been highly concentrated in a few hands (the DeGaullist presidency being the most recent). If
we choose this as the equilibrium situation toward which French politics
tends to return, studies can be directed to discover the *outside* factors that
upset the equilibrium and set in train another cyclical movement away from,
then toward, concentrated authority and control. It is equally plausible,
though perhaps more difficult, to select years of dispersed power as the equilibrium state and proceed from there. The model can be modified by incorporating into it some factors that are labeled *outside* (exogenous) in the
original exercise.

It is also feasible to treat any relatively steady period as an equilibrium
and to search for factors that account for movements away from or toward
reinstating the pattern. In any case, the maximization postulate suggests that
any well-developed model for investigation must connect value expectations
and realizations with its significant features. The controlling decisionmakers
will not act in harmony with these features unless they expect to be relatively better off, in terms of relevant value demands, by conforming rather
than by failing to do so. Over a period of time we assume that expectations
must be reenforced by at least some value realizations. The equilibrium
model must be sufficiently refined to show which perspectives are perceived
as gratified in the process. If changes are to be fully accounted for, any dis-
equilibria generated by internal or external factors must be traceable to discrepancies between perspectives and operations (of those who have the
effective assets to influence outcomes). Whether changes are cyclical or
structural, they call for appropriate shifts in perspectives and in operational
activity.

It is not necessary to postpone scientific inquiry on a decision process
until satisfactory theoretical constructs are available or until adequate data
are gathered to meet all requirements. Selected situations can be illuminated
by partial studies. Useful empirical research can be directed to one of the
seven decision functions.

For instance, it may be possible to identify cyclical tendencies in the behavior of those who are identified with a function. Perhaps it can be found that the planning components of the *intelligence* function tend to gravitate into the hands of a few planners, and that this is followed by the mobilization of political groups to reassert themselves against the intelligence or planning bureaucracy. The bureaucracy may announce reforms by including more consultation, after which the initial state is gradually restored. Studies of *promotion* may indicate that tendencies toward bossism in the party system may be counteracted by promotional factions that succesfully, if temporarily, activate the party membership. Study of *prescriptive* structures may indicate that the tendency in legislative bodies to concentrate control in the hands of a few committees can be held in check by initiatives that for a time restore all committees to their previous role. If police policies (part of *invocation*) fall into the hands of the detective branch of the service, and concentrate yet further in a small number of officers, a countervailing movement may stimulate a period of wider participation by more detectives and also by officials from other branches of the police. If administrative controls (the *application* function) are concentrated in military rather than civilian agencies, the civilian bureaus and departments may form complex coalitions that spread effective control once more for a while. If *terminating* agencies come into the hands of officials identified with some expropriated interests, an answering coalition of interests may restore the earlier state. If the *appraisal* function is dominated by particularly censorious and rebellious groups, officials who represent less disaffected elements may reassert themselves.

If any one of these cyclical oscillations is examined in depth, the results will probably corroborate hypotheses inspired by the maximization postulate. Initial changes may occur when groups that were previously active in the context fail to make themselves visible and effective in the decision process at the points of commitment. This phenomenon is especially evident in the aftermath of reform movements—as for the removal of pollution, for instance. These movements may have mobilized enough influence to produce structural or functional innovations. Then, perhaps, reformers discontinued research and publication concerned with the deleterious consequences of pollution. Active pressure may be reinstated by the publication of new research results.

The highly generalized model of the political process—inspired by the social process analysis—can be set forth as follows:

The sharing of power increases	*The sharing of power decreases*
if effective participants *expect* net value indulgences (and) if expectations are *realized*	if effective participants *expect* net value indulgences (and) if expectations are *not realized*

By *Effective participants* is meant the combination of individuals and groups, organized or unorganized, who control the base values required to innovate, maintain, or destroy the system. *Expectations* refer to subjective events; and it is to be noted that all values, not simply power, are at stake. Strictly speaking, the next component—value *realizations*—is unnecessary. However, experience and analysis both suggest that subjective events are affected by the degree to which the environment gratifies or fails to gratify expectations. Hence the theoretical model is complicated in order to bring it closer to the situations to be examined.

Without pursuing the point in detail, we may note the fact that in different situations it will presumably be necessary or convenient for an investigator of power changes to work with indices of varying degrees of refinement. The most differentiated indication of perspectives are the *words* (and word equivalents) uttered by a participant. More democracy may be predicted, for instance, if more members of the community assert their desire for it and their conviction that they will be better off with democratic than with antidemocratic systems. If direct utterances are not accessible, perspectives may be less directly indicated by means of the *content of the communication programs that come to the focus of community attention*. It often seems reasonable to assume that expectations follow the news. Often the most available indicators are a step more remote, as when environmental changes are defined by the analyst as favorable or not (without demonstrating in detail that they have come to community attention and have been referred to as favorable). If a nondemocratic form of government coincides with defeat, the body politic may be expected to become more democratic on the assumption that defeat is perceived as deprivational for nondemocracy, hence relatively favorable for democracy. In summary:

Expectations = Directly indicated by words (and word equivalents)
  or
  Indirectly indicated by words (and word equivalents)
  at the focus of attention

or

> Less directly indicated by nonverbal changes in the environment

Expectations are fundamental to microscopic as well as to macroscopic analyses of the factors affecting decision. What is implied when we speak of the bureaucratizing tendencies of large organizations? Such an interpretation is open to confirmation or disconfirmation in concrete circumstances, as when proposed innovations are turned down because most of the controlling officials fear that their power will be cut down by change. If innovations are accepted, research must be able to demonstrate that alternatives were perceived as more dangerous still.

The study of *organization* calls for serializing the component situations that comprise the structure. If all the vertical and horizontal components are taken into account, these situations are numerous. The components are differentiated according to the degree of centralization-decentralization, concentration-separation, formal and informal participation, and so on. Detailed analysis carries us to the familiar face-to-face exchange of value indulgences and deprivations in every subsituation (as perceived by participants who are variously identified with the organization or with substructures and rivals, and who are concerned with the value demands and expectations salient to each identification). Explanatory hypotheses can be coordinated into equilibrium models devised on static or dynamic assumptions.

The political structure as a whole can be taken as the phenomenon to be explained. The numerous hypotheses suggested by experience and the maximization postulate can be integrated into analytic models which are intended to guide scientific research.

Projection

In an important sense scientific analysis is backward looking. At any given moment anyone whose assertions are challenged wants to be able to reply by summarizing past (even though recent) data that appear to confirm the relevant generalizations within narrow limits. In controversial situations the accent is on verification, and the results are most conclusive when they deal with elapsed events. The attempt to be more and more certain about the validity of an empirical proposition leads scientists to focus more and more narrowly on a selected category of events.

Policy, on the other hand, looks toward the future. And the future, like the past, is contextual. Can implicit maps of expectation about future developments be rendered more explicit and dependable? This is the distinctive challenge of the fourth intellectual task in a problem-oriented approach. The future is projected by assuming for a moment that what the individual or the organization can do will make no significant difference in the outcome.

Some decisionmakers and observers find it distasteful to imagine, even momentarily, that they are missing as influential components of the process. Even the stipulation that for purposes of the exercise they are presumed to act routinely (that is, as they have in the past) is not always sufficient concession to the inner demand to feel salient at all times. But such an exercise in suspended judgment wins acceptance as its advantages are experienced. It may become abundantly clear that existing policies are bound to fail, but that many elements in the context are open to change if it be assumed that present policies are even slightly modified.

Only in recent years has it been accepted that the study of the future is a creditable intellectual activity. Especially in its earlier years modern scientists struggled against astrologers, alchemists, palmists, and a host of rivals who purported to discover and explain past and future events. The ideology of science was "antimystical," "antisupernatural," "antispiritual." It preferred problems that could be dealt with in mass-energy terms, and until the discovery of discontinuities (generalized by Planck), simple models of causality were in the ascendancy. The bias was that x could not be treated as a cause of y unless the observer could describe the path of x and y. There must be no "action at a distance," hence no mysterious jumps. The remodeled conception has been subsumed under a theory of "statistical causation," meaning that if the pattern at x^1 could be observed and the pattern of x^2 could be predicted and replicated, a causal connection could be inferred. This in theory came about because some micro-phenomena were too small to measure at all points along their paths, and also because the paths might change abruptly. Some macro-phenomena also required a similar model.

The scientific observer who focuses on life has adopted an even more complex image of the world. Instead of searching for mass-energy equivalents, he has discovered the importance of examining the transmission of information, which calls for descriptions that emphasize pattern rather than quantity. The most significant fact about a genetic message, or the transmission of nerve impulse, or radio-wave dissemination for communication purposes, is not the amount of energy utilized but the arrangement of the events constituting the process. In the study of human affairs by scientific methods, it also becomes clear that *symbols* as well as information *bits* are predictively useful, and that they involve more complex patterns than information. A symbol event *refers,* and among the references are those alluding to future events (more concretely, to preferences, determinations, and identities). The discovery that by finding how people refer to the past, present, and future the observer can improve his predictions of their conduct has brought about a further attenuation of the "billiard-ball" metaphor of yesterday's conceptions of scientific explanation.

Since decisions depend to such a degree on expectations about the future, it has become increasingly evident that these assumptions should be subject to methodological discipline. Hence the contextual principle has been applied to the critical assessment of the results obtained by various procedures. One procedure is the *extrapolation* of sequences. In the world arena as a whole, for instance, it is possible to project two expanding power groups and to see that they are on a collision course which is likely to culminate at a given time and place.

Such provisional extrapolations are open to evaluation in the light of current scientific knowledge of the factors that *condition* the outcome of such conflicts. When this evaluation is systematically done, the resulting estimates of the future provide a more trustworthy basis of inference than before. New contingency models may be formulated for the future. These may drastically modify the initial extrapolation by suggesting, for instance, that Japan is likely to alter the outcome of Soviet-American relations.

It is also recognized that *experienced judgment* is a source of estimates that it would be foolish to ignore. Efforts have been made to obtain expert judgment in a statistically satisfactory sample. In this connection scientific curiosity has turned toward the study of forecasters and predictors in the hope of isolating factors that condition success.

Alternatives

Finally we come to the pay-off function in a problem-oriented approach. If goals are to be optimalized, what strategies are most advantageous for achieving the objectives sought?

We speak of the fifth intellectual task as though it were a single problem-solving component. In the most general sense this is so. Yet such a statement greatly simplifies the many interrelated patterns involved: the invention of policy proposals; a comparative evaluation in terms of short- and long-term benefits, costs, and risks; the making of a final commitment.

A generalized set of questions is a preliminary guide to the operation:

1. Whose policy goals are to be realized?

The first step in examining policy alternatives is to make sure that explicit assumptions are made about the identity of the effective decisionmakers. The policy scientist either adopts the perspectives of some other participant in the context or acts on his own.

2. What is the problem or set of problems in hand?

Problems vary enormously in value scope and range. By definition a problem is a perceived discrepancy between goals and an actual or anticipated state of affairs. The first awareness of a problem may originate with a policy scientist who is exploring connections between proclaimed aims and factual circumstances. More commonly, however, direct participants discover a problem and begin to think or do something about it.

3. What particularized objectives are sought to be realized through the policy process?

Objectives are defined in reference to the goal values presumed to be made effective in the context. Although we have called for the specification of goal values, it is not uncommon to discover that goal values are erratically formulated. The political myth may ostensibly be stated in documents that vary in level of abstraction from the most inclusive to the very specific. Usually there are ambiguities that must be overcome if objectives are to be critically considered.

4. Assuming that objectives p^1 (p^2, etc.) can be realized, what is the probability that they will optimalize the results sought?

This requires an analysis of middle- and long-range effects of hypothetical decisions in the social process.

5. What decision outcomes are most adequate to the effects sought? Who decides what and how?

The decision outcomes may refer to one or all of the seven phases of the power process of one or more levels in the transnational, national, or subnational community. The decisionmakers may be located in one or several structures and may be predisposed to proceed in ascertainable ways.

6. What predispositions are favorable, unfavorable, or noncommittal in reference to the outcomes as presently formulated? Are they sufficient to obtain the decision sought (assuming little effort to mobilize support)?

Is it probable that predispositions will be sufficiently strong (at a future time, owing to conditions beyond the manipulator's control) to affect the result conclusively and with little regard to the initiatives of the decision-maker?

7. What strategies will optimalize value goals? What is the probability of a successful outcome? The strategies will be considered in the light of various contingencies and predispositions (self, opponents, allies, noncommitted). The various instruments of policy (diplomatic, ideological, economic, military) will be utilized independently or jointly.

Models of a problem-solving process, like models of the social context, can be carried to any degree of refinement required by problem solving in concrete situations. The fundamental intellectual tasks remain, whether the emphasis is on content or procedure. (For the Dror model see page 169 below.)

The policy sciences are particularly concerned with the problem solving performance of governmental and private organizations. As we have indicated the policy scientist is concerned with every dimension of the internal and external relationship between any organization and its environing context. This implies special emphasis on policy appraisal, whether executed for a client or as a citizen who is directly involved in public decisions.

The appraisal responsibility of a policy scientist may take several forms, among which the following may be provisionally identified:

The Ordinary Policy Process. One appraisal task is to examine the ordinary decision process (intelligence, promotion, prescription, invocation, application, termination, appraisal).

The Constitutive Policy Process. Constitutive decisions maintain or alter the allocation of authority and control.

Particular or *aggregate* decisions are subject to appraisal. The former is a single outcome; the latter a series of outcomes, selected according to area, period or function.

The preceding categories refer to *process* appraisal, since they deal with the internal functioning of the ordinary or constitutive decision process. *Impact* appraisal is focussed on the relationship between policy goals and the social or resources context.

CHAPTER 4

Diversity: Synthesis of Methods

Introduction

We have identified the twofold responsibility of the policy sciences as analyzing and improving the policy process itself and as expeditirg the mobilization of knowledge pertinent to specific policies. Policy scientists will undoubtedly emphasize one or the other objective at different stages of their careers. Political scientists and public lawyers are likely to begin with the structural problems of government, and to acquire expertness in a particular range of policy issues, such as those relating to weapon technology, space research, or oceanography. The movement of scientists and engineers may be in the opposite direction, beginning with technical knowledge relevent to policies in a specific field and acquiring expertness in the decision process as they go along.

In view of the complexity and diversity of policy processes it is safe to predict that, as the policy sciences evolve, the scope of the field will be variously interpreted, and that techniques will be invented and adapted to meet many needs. Practitioners will start with the methods with which they are most familiar. Engineers, for example, usually seek to transfer tightly formalized models and quantitative procedures to policy problems. Lawyers and social scientists are typically less impressed with the relevance of such methods to the realities of advice and consent. In any case, it is probable that the self-correcting impact of experience will modify and integrate diverse approaches.

If the policy processes are to be competently explored, it will be necessary to employ methods of observation that require at least some analysts to relate themselves closely to the research field. This requirement that some analysts function as participant observers to the policy process must be variously interpreted to fit contrasting circumstances. It is not altogether applicable to historical inquiry, although a false image of historians is perpetuated if we overlook the degree to which they must cultivate the good will of

58

the custodians of family papers or of donors who make funds available for travel and record making. It must be recognized also that many analysts of the current stream of decision can make themselves relevant without penetrating the most sensitive arenas.

To the degree that policy scientists become involved with theoretical and empirical studies of current decisions, they are cross-pressured by those who are exposed to the exigencies of political, administrative, military, and related responsibilities. The scientific role emphasizes explanatory models and techniques of data gathering and processing that provide grist for the formal system. Activists, and those who identify with or are dependent on activists, are tempted to abandon the often onerous requirements of theory and data gathering. The task is to devise research programs that combine dependable techniques of investigation with a degree of participatory activity in the problem-solving process.

In a science-saturated society it is unnecessary to recapitulate the generally accepted methods of theory construction, experimental design, and the like. Nor is it the present purpose to present an introductory manual suitable to instruction in specific areas, such as administrative management, systems analysis, or operations research. Rather, the aim is to call attention to some technical approaches that have already appeared in partial answer to the requirements of contextuality and problem orientation. These pages will be amplified in subsequent chapters that deal directly with the professional role of the policy scientist and with the instruments adapted to instructional purposes.

Since complexity is a recurring theme of all who give serious thought to public policy, it is not surprising to find that some of the most interesting technical innovations or adaptations are intended to cope with complexity, and with the future-oriented, exploratory, and creative dimensions of the policy process. We therefore focus on "contextual mapping," "developmental constructs," "prototyping technique," and "incorporating computer simulation." (The discussion of "participant observation" is deferred.)

Far from denying or minimizing complexity, the policy sciences emphasize complication, and search for ways of improving insight, understanding, and control. Full recognition is given to the fact that individual decision-makers are subject to severe constraints, and that, for instance, whatever one does must be accomplished in the straitjacket of time. (Unhappily, borrowed time is a fantasy; there is only better use of time.)

It is, in fact, this stress on time that distinguishes urban civilized man from rustic, tribal, or primitive man. The more visible the interdependencies in the social process, the more implacable and exhaustible time appears to be. Primitive men were evidently in some confusion and uncertainty about the boundary between life and death. On the whole, they tended to believe that the soul, the conscious primary ego, continued after death and perhaps occupied successive bodies in the same way that one resides temporarily in camps. In any case, the time available to each individual was not the ephemeral moment in the evolution of the cosmos that it now seems to be.

That time is an asset in pathetically short supply has aroused an intense determination among many civilized men to conquer death and to extend human life indefinitely. No human beings have sought immortality with more passionate intensity than the men who have had access to the greatest value indulgences open to human beings. For many emperors and kings the fact of death has seemed to be a supreme insult, a tragic joke, a cosmic provocation. We read of the fantastic lengths to which some men of power have gone—how they surrounded themselves with whoever had the arrogance to claim a key to the mystery of death; how they squandered the resources of an empire on laboratories and explorations in search of the spring of perpetual youth; how they drank the blood of the young, the strong, and the beautiful in desperate pursuit of time.

Paradoxically, the end of individual death is in sight at the very moment that mankind is facing the threat of instant collective annihilation. One line of scientific advance emphasizes the possibility of locating molecules as they show signs of wear, and replacing them indefinitely. Another approach stresses the genetic instruments soon to be perfected for remodeling the structure of higher forms of life, and including in the genetic directives from one generation to the next instructions that extend self-maintaining tactics indefinitely. There is also the machine builder, not simply the simulator of living forms, but the architect of machines complex enough to provide for self-repair. And, of course, there are modest programs that promise no more than to add to the traditional threescore and ten years of life a doubled or tripled span.

So far as policy scientists are concerned, the prospect of abolishing death is a contingency of the long-range type which they are prepared to consider far in advance of its full realization. In fact, no problem is more intriguing than the policy questions that present themselves if life is substantially lengthened or stretched out indefinitely. Man's institutions have always been based on the expectation of death in the sense that individuals are assumed to undergo a change of state that terminates at least one career. Whatever the long-range future of secular immortality, the policy scientists of our time will continue to deal with human beings who expect to live briefly and whose most obvious asset for policy purposes is capacity to focus attention on problems. *From one point of view, the principal strategy of the policy sciences can be summed up as guiding the focus of attention of all participants in decision.*

The strategy of guiding individual or collective attention is no simple matter. The most obvious constraint is that people spend a third of their life asleep. This flat statement is open to qualification, since it depends on response to climatic and seasonal factors, as well as to more direct sociopersonal determiners. Individuals differ greatly from one period of life to another in their demand for sleep, and they differ in the amount of sleep required. Every society makes use of drugs to induce, defer, or affect the quality of sleep. In some circles it is predicted that mankind can presently be freed from sleep, regarding it as an anachronistic pattern adapted to a very different environment.

Apart from sleep, the focus of attention of many, if not most, people is highly autistic. *Autism* is a mode of internalization. Daydreaming may actually be more vivid (more real) than the immediate environment. Hence there are inner barriers to be overcome if full waking attention is to be captured for news, comment, and commitment to common problems. The stream of inner fantasy appears to provide a symbolically stable private environment, enabling the individual to obtain enough satisfaction from the regular routines of living to keep him active as a functioning student, housewife, worker, or manager. The ordinary expressions required in everyday social intercourse can be carried on automatically, and with little distraction from the inner cinema. (Not much attention need be mobilized to exchange everyday greetings, to comment on the weather, to recount a few physical symptoms or established gripes, and to handle highly stylized tasks with or without the aid of machines.)

The overwhelming deluge of radio and television programs and of print has generated self-protective responses from the millions of viewers, listeners, and readers. Audience members have learned to live in a state of *selective inattention,* and to disregard most of what is technically accessible. Attention flickers and turns away, and the stream of inner fantasy rolls on.

Presumably these mechanisms operate as *defenses against anxiety.* Anxiety is acute dysphoria. A stab of anxiety may be accompanied by irregular breathing, heart action, sweating, and other bodily signs of tension. In fact, the omnipresent role of anxiety is a clue to the astonishing uniformity of human conduct. Behavioral uniformity is maintained by sustaining an inner life that is relatively free of anxiety. This is accomplished by means of selective inattention to whatever interferes with the perpetual flow of inner moods and images. Impulses or perceptions of the outer environment that tend to arouse anxiety are automatically turned off, not on. Hence the threat of anxiety is the sanctioning device by which the conscience acts to protect itself against unwelcome impulses, thoughts, feelings, and consummated deeds. By *conscience* is meant all the norms of conduct acquired during early years of development. Typically these norms are the result of compromises among competing or conflicting impulses, and they are defended by the conscience with promptitude and intensity.

Neither the military nor the police forces of society could possibly muster strong enough forces to cope with a universal breakdown of conscience in an entire community. "Inner police" are essential to public and private stability, and these inner monitors operate chiefly by the threat and use of anxiety. Private fantasies are the compromise formations by which the individual is able to obtain partial sources of continuing gratification without arousing the conscience or even noticing many unwelcome phenomena in the environment—hence the general disposition to ignore disturbing news or commet, or to dismiss and neutralize unwelcome messages by the mechanisms of forgetting, denial, substitution of fantasied wish fulfillments, and so on.

We have been accounting for selective inattention. Sometimes policy scientists must take note of the opposite extremes of *obsessive preoccupation, wild excitement,* and *disorganized behavior.* The previous paragraphs have hinted at the explosive propensities of human beings that lie hidden from notice in ordinary intercrisis situations. As with all explosive potentials, it is often puzzling to fit a modest trigger to a tremendous detonation. Studies of riots comment with monotonous regularity on the relative triviality of the critical incident that touched off ensuing hours or days of arson, burglary, rape, and killing.

In the long history of civilization we are accustomed to recognize periods of acquiescence modified by rejection. It is easy to concentrate on the dramatic upheavals and to emphasize the nonreflective, impulsive, and destructive features of revolution, whether the reference is to a time of troubles in the history of China, or the peasant revolts or urban revolutions in Western Europe. There is no denying the passion of the crowd or the mob, and there is no disposition to claim that under the circumstances people are acting other than nonrationally (if we understand this term to mean that behavior is impulsive and nonreflective). The policy sciencies can reasonably inquire into the factors that precipitate such behavior and take as a manipulative task the discovery of the *means by which all who participate in a policy-*

forming and policy-executing process can live up to their potential for sound judgment.

It should be stressed at this point that calmness is no guarantee of sound judgment. For that matter, the opposite of calmness—fervor or disruption —is no guarantee of judgment. The cultivation of an etiquette of casualness may be combined with the fundamental indifference of the noninvolved, and the eventual result of such a decision process may be disastrous—disastrous, that is, in the sense that lives and property are destroyed in an orgiastic explosion generated by deprivation and alienation.

The inference is that sound, realistic judgment is no automatic consequence of "cooling it" or of "confrontation." In view of the long record of milennial dreams and episodic disenchantment it is not unreasonable to conclude that the syndrome of revolutionary violence, like the institution of war, is likely to continue until the conditions that cause it are removed. If such primitive strategies of change are to be superseded, the policy processes of society must be changed. Obviously the policy sciences will hope to acquire the knowledge necessary to foster social change with minimum reliance on coercive instrumentalities. And this may call for deliberate strategies to destroy calmness in time to obviate calamity.

A fundamental question, then, is *how to mobilize enough attention on the relevant context to further the consideration of common policy problems without promoting a situation in which realistic consideration is impossible.* The net value advantage of participating in the policy process must be higher than the advantages of nonparticipation (or of participation in disruptive ways). At any given moment the predispositions of those who decide must be ready to focus on a common map and to act in ways that facilitate the problem-solving process. In no small measure present predispositions are a function of pay-offs from past attentive behavior.

If the policy sciences are to succeed, they must explore every method that could conceivably contribute to their contextual and problem-oriented responsibility. Many of the methods devised for policy sciences research, when perfected and adapted, will probably diffuse widely among the deciding and choosing processes of public and civic order.

Contextual Mapping

If the focus of attention of participants in the policy process is to have access to a comprehensive, concise, and dependable image of the context, appropriate procedures must be invented for the purpose. Important steps have already been taken in this direction. As usual, it turns out that most of the specific patterns adapted to the task are already in existence, and that understanding and experience are both needed to bring the pieces together.

Our discussion of contextuality drew attention to the role of comprehensive conceptions of the social process and of the several phases of decision. The analysis of problem solving identified five intellectual tasks that direct attention to five modes of viewing, and hence of presenting, the relevant context. The present topic is concerned with procedures by which these interrelated aspects can be most effectively brought to the focus of attention of participants in decision. Presumably the decisionmakers who are closest to the use of contextual mapping are connected with the intelligence (planning) and appraisal phases of the total process.

Contextual mapping requires *continuity* or the expectation of working together over a substantial period. In this way there is an opportunity to explore the rough contours of a map in detail, and to minimize the repetitions and superficialities inseparable from dealing from scratch with a procession of strangers.

Another specification is *small numbers*. We know that a small committee can interact more quickly and with less reserve than is likely with assemblies and conventions.

A third feature is *environmental continuity*. This is a less stringent requirement than small size, since arrangements can be made to transport exhibits from place to place. There are, however, advantages in a setting where everybody feels at home.

A further specification is extensive use of *audio-visual and related aids* in the form of charts, maps, and exhibits. These auxiliary materials can be systematically arranged in the room to serve as a reminder of the social process context as perceived in each problem-solving perspective. A principal advantage of audio-visual aids is that they add a dimension of precision and vividness that is often missed by persons who are not fully at home with equations. The maps and charts act as information storage and retrieval aids, since those who participate in group deliberations use visual cues to recall the gist of past discussions.

A critical point is full *personal participation* in the process by group members. Everyone is expected to prepare and present contributions to the common enterprise. No one is allowed to play the role of a delphic oracle, whose prestige depends on unwillingness to reveal himself as a fellow enquirer.

This does not preclude *witnesses* or *servicing* of the group by staff. It may seem useful to supplement the group by inviting an occasional expert to appear. The group can also benefit by staff work to assist in the preparation of the audio-visual features of the presentations, or to take responsibility for finding a satisfactory means of preparing a chart or map to clarify a point that arose in discussion.

The agenda should be *spiral*. One advantage of the policy sciences approach is comprehensiveness. If it is to be fully realized, group procedures must be planned to make sure that the process model and the problem-solving tasks are systematically covered. The tendency of every group is to narrow its frame of reference, chiefly because quick and easy individual payoffs so frequently come by adding minor and rather obvious amplifications to the field of common reference. Hence the focus of attention needs to be redirected to neglected areas. If deliberations have been preoccupied with wealth and power, for instance, group members may take responsibility for considering possible repercussions on other values. Similarly the group may be so absorbed in the present and in the immediate future that it has forgotten about the past. An examination of past trends may suggest a novel potentiality for the future, or call attention to conditioning factors that have been overlooked.

Contextual mapping can *evaluate and utilize sophisticated procedures* such as the computer makes possible. The programmer is a key assistant in the employment of computers to simulate past, present, and future events.

Contextual mapping requires a *comprehensive schematic view* of the entire social process, and of the role of the decision process within it. The procedure also calls for the systematic presentation of modified maps that fulfill each of the intellectual tasks concerned with the problem-solving approach.

In governmental institutions contextual mapping is seldom done at the highest level. However, it has been adapted to major problems in limited sectors. The most resource-consuming instances appear in connection with the planning and execution of military campaigns, such as the landing of Allied men and equipment from Great Britain on the continent of Europe in World War II. Every potential landing place was described in detail and simulated in exact exercise models. Audio-visual presentations were available for critical discussion and gaming purposes.

In recent years the technique of contextual mapping has been extended from the military to other spheres of policy. However, the tendency has been to adapt these techniques to training purposes rather than to top policy simulation. (We discuss the "decision seminar" technique as an instructional device in chapter 8.)

Contextual mapping has been partially fitted to the requirements of policy research, and it is clear that the procedure can be adapted to this purpose without waiting to be totally incorporated in government. For instance, it is possible to strengthen both science and policy by developing a network of *counterpart seminars* in any body politic where inquiry and discussion are relatively free.

What is involved can be described by imagining a network of counterpart seminars organized in connection with professional schools, colleges, and other private associations. One set of counterpart seminars can parallel selected official and semiofficial *structures* of government. Among the agencies specialized to the *intelligence* function are planning commissions at the municipal, state, national, or transnational level. The *promotional* structures include the executive bodies of the political parties or pressure groups. Among the *prescribing* organs are the principal committees of legislative bodies. The *invoking* function is the principal task of the office of the police or the prosecuting authorities. *Application* functions (which are the final characterization of a concrete set of facts in terms of prescriptions) are carried out by administrative commissions, courts, and department heads. *Termination* operations involve the cancellation of legislative and other prescriptions, and the adjustment of the resulting claims for compensation or relocation. Housing authorities use special agencies for these tasks. The *appraisal* function is executed by commissions of inquiry that evaluate the degree to which policy directives have been put into effect and the allocation of responsibility for success or failure.

A counterpart seminar that parallels a given structure of government seeks to clarify the goals appropriate to the assessment of the agency involved. The seminar gathers data that make it possible to describe trends toward realizing, or failing to realize, these goals. The group undertakes to explain the factors that account for the success or failure of the decision process to yield appropriate results. Projections are made of the probable future of the structure and of its level of effectiveness. Policy alternatives are invented or evaluated that might enable the agency to improve its future performance. The seminar might decide to invent strategies of its own for the purpose of influencing the official structure in question. In this case the seminar projects the probable success or failure of its own efforts, and analyzes the feedback through time of its own activities.

Counterpart seminars may be organized in reference to a function rather than a structure. For example, a *functional counterpart seminar* might deal with one of the seven categories mentioned above (intelligence, promotion, prescription, invocation, application, termination, appraisal) and follow it through the governmental process at the national, transnational, or subnational level. The structures mentioned before as relatively specialized to each function neither monopolize the performance of a function nor fail to perform other functions themselves. Investigation shows that to some extent every official structure necessarily performs every function to some extent, and that the degree of participation in the function varies through time.

A third possibility is the organization of *counterpart problem seminars.* They focus on a task that cuts across structures and functions, such as improving the level of security in the world community, or of obtaining and retaining appropriately motivated and capable personnel for public services.

The counterpart seminar is one of the most promising means of disciplining the analytic models of scientific tradition by examining their explanatory relevancy through the emerging future, and of integrating the analytic task with the other four intellectual tasks of a problem-oriented approach.

Developmental Constructs

One of the most radical and promising departures in the evolution of the policy sciences is a technique at once adapted to examining the present conjuncture of events, and to giving full weight to the axis of time. The reference is to *developmental constructs.* The essential purpose is to enable the policy analyst, and hopefully the decisionmaker, to find his way in the complexities of the total situation in which he operates. The preparation of a developmental construct does not ignore complexity; it proposes an orderly way of revealing the significant contours of reality.

The nature of the technique can be most quickly grasped by indicating how it compares or contrasts with the way in which Karl Marx formulated the assertion that our historical epoch is characterized by the movement from capitalism to socialism, hence, in power terms, the passage of power from the bourgeoisie to the proletariat.

First, here are some points of similarity. The Marxist model concentrates on *fundamental features of the total context* with which Marx was concerned. Lesser features were de-emphasized as a means of concentrating attention on value shaping and sharing, and on basic social institutions.

A second characteristic of the Marxist model is implied: it describes important states of affairs in the past and future, and hence *provides criteria for examining contemporary changes as movements toward or away from the selected initial or terminal patterns.*

A third point is that a construct is *prepared in the light of available knowledge and continually appraised as knowledge expands.* Marx was a brilliant scholar who subjected himself to the discipline of examining the physical, biological, and cultural disciplines of his day. His monumental formulation was no fruit of elementary wish-fulfillment.

We come now to the differences between the techniques and the partial approximation exemplified by Marx. First, the construct is *tentative and exploratory,* not dogmatic. Words that refer to future events are inferences from the existing supply of scientific and historical knowledge, and of provisional projections. They are not, however, science. They do not conjoin theory and data, since data are not available about the future. The data are predicted, not summarized. Above all, a construct is not dogmatically held. It is not said to be inevitable. It is not even put forward with the primary purpose of forecasting; rather, the construct is understood to afford a present modification of communicated events at the focus of attention. A future consequence may be the initiation of acts that prevent a forecast from coming true. This is the problem-solving demand to "create" or "invent" the future, not to remain passively contented with the forecasting role.

Perhaps it is worth underlining the point that developmental constructs *explicitly distinguish preferential from probability models.* The goal of human dignity can be specified as a preference model for the future of man. But insofar as the next few decades are concerned, the most likely future may be far short of the goal. By insisting on the importance of separating the goal from projective models, the danger is diminished that conviction will seriously warp realistic judgment. We are justified in viewing with reserve all models of the future that show the future *is* as congruous with the formulator's *ought.*

These cautions do not, however, imply that preference models cannot perform a realistic and creative role in the performance of the fifth intellectual task referred to before. Take, for example, the world models project of the World Law Fund. The goal is to assist in moving the world toward a situation in which world public order is peaceful and increasingly compatible with all the objectives of human dignity. Part of the task is to clarify the policy sequence by which probable contingencies can be met in ways that increase the likelihood that the goal will be approached.

If such an exercise is to be most helpful, and to enlist the interest of participants from some countries, it is important to lay aside the consideration of drastic contingencies of two kinds: *(a)* the occurrence of nuclear holocaust and *(b)* the conquest of the globe by one superpower bloc. The postulate should also be explicit that for purposes of the exercise the preference is held to be possible of realization. As the inclusive model refers to successive future periods, the factual contingencies assumed must be close enough to accepted expectations of what is possible so that the whole enterprise is taken seriously.

As the developmental construct is formed, it ought to undergo the discipline of being exposed to intermittent evaluation. From time to time in future years the general model should be systematically reconsidered in the light of recent developments and of new knowledge.

Prototyping Technique

Among the methods in process of adaptation to the needs of the policy sciences is the technique of *prototyping*. It is to be distinguished, on the one hand, from the technique of *experimentation,* and, on the other, from controversial *intervention* in the decision processes of a territorial or pluralistic group.

The extraordinary success achieved by the physical and biological sciences has given great prestige to the experimental procedures on which they so extensively rely. Hence modern social and behavioral sciences have been at great pains to attempt to transform themselves into disciplines based on the results of experimentation. This aspiration has been partly realized in some branches of psychology and small group research. A fully experimental technique is able to design a research whose variables are identified and measured, so that it is feasible to vary the mix of factors and to observe the results as replicated.

The policy scientist is typically confronted by problem situations in which the principal question is how to compare policy objectives and strategies in terms of causes and consequences. Hence his attention is focused, not only on highly specific, known, and measurable variables, but on institutional practices. We define a practice as a pattern of perspectives and operations that is typically specialized to the shaping and sharing of a class of values. Policy questions usually entail the evaluation of existing or potential practices according to the net value impacts. Such questions range from the most fundamental constitutive matters, such as the relative significance of private capitalism or socialism for wealth, power, and other values, to less profound issues.

The technique of prototyping, then, *emphasizes institutional practices more than a known list of measurable variables*. The contrast must not be exaggerated, since every practice is a composite of variables and can be partially described by indicators of their pattern and magnitude. The *perspec-*

tives included in a given practice are the identities, demands, and expectations of those who are usually involved with it. The *operations* defined as components of a practice are behavioral routines such as externalized or internalized acts, or acts of resource or sign manipulation. The policy scientist utilizes the measuring techniques of the experimenter, but these are subordinated to the configuration of pertinent practices. The experimenter, on the contrary, is driven by a demand to imagine every conceivable situation in which the variable changes in a predictable way and to demonstrate the full range in the laboratory.

A second mark of prototyping is its *subordination to enlightenment rather than power*. It is controlled by specialists on knowledge rather than power. In the context the scientist uses available power as a base for enlightenment, not vice versa. The situation ceases to be a prototype if it becomes a controversial issue among rivals in the pertinent power arenas. The requirements of the technique can be clarified by referring to two instances of prototyping. In one case an anthropologist stepped into the top power position in a traditional "feudal" estate, where the patron was authorized to employ the labor force (some of the time) for his own advantage. The scientist decided to use Vicos (in the Peruvian Andes) as a field study in strategies of modernization. Hence the anthropologist-boss sought to change some of the technologies of production and to improve the realism of the local decision process. Preinnovation, innovation, and postinnovation phases were described by a number of well-known data-gathering methods.

The other prototype was evolved in a psychiatric hospital. Unlike Vicos, there was no one person who made up his mind to try out new treatment practices and who was able to proceed accordingly. The decision was made by the staff and involved no outside pressure or public controversy. Vicos, too, did not at first become involved in the controversies of the larger national arena of Peru. If the scientist had lost control of the innovation, the situation would have moved from prototyping to direct political intervention.

An important feature of prototyping is the preparation of experienced people who can carry similar innovations to other places if they are accepted as promising. Typically, an important component of social change is the presence of *leaders* who have achieved self-confidence in their aims and techniques. In the initial stages, at least, before extensive publications are prepared, firsthand experience is the principal source of the necessary outlook.

It is not implied that unanimity of aim and strategy must include the entire community or association. It is only necessary to begin with a consensus that includes willingness among the most effective participants to give the innovation a fair test. Most social innovations must build supporting motivations after they have been introduced. In fact, the chief purpose of a prototype is to see whether the innovation is capable of accomplishing this among other results. The *introductory phase of tentative agreement is the only special condition required by prototyping.*

Technical problems arise in attempting to identify the degree of initial acceptance that justifies asserting that a practice has been introduced and that postintroduction events are to be treated as consequences. At Vicos the project was past the first stage after the scientist-boss won the acquiscent support of the manager and the leading elders of the community to plan together. At the Yale Psychiatric Institute the project—which was designed to study the effects of sharing power with the patients and junior staff—could be described as introduced, when a few patient-staff meetings were actually held.

Usually the initial prototype includes some features that are judged by the policy scientists involved to be mistaken interpretations of what was to be tried out. Therefore some acts are judged to be clumsy though useful steps in clarifying a practice or a strategy of innovation. Occasionally a fortunate accident contributes to the success of a project and must be discounted in appraising the sequence of events.

Since it is not cut and dried in advance, prototyping opens the door to continued learning and creativity. It therefore lends itself to continuing self-appraisal and policy invention. Both the Vicos and the YPI prototypes generated a wide range of proposals for future strategists of power sharing.

In a given undertaking the scientist's eagerness to obtain conclusive results may lead to negative consequences. He may, for example, unduly interfere with the situation by the specific techniques that are utilized to permit appraisals to be made. Some projects suffer from the demand to document what has happened to a degree that produces hostility and withdrawal on the part of the "guinea pigs." A continuing problem is how to gain the cooperation needed for documentation without arousing resentment. Two recurring questions are always pertinent, therefore, to a proposed item or mode of evaluation. How necessary are these data to evaluating the model? How great is the cost (in all categories) of obtaining such information?

The exploratory function of a prototype allows it to be the first step in a program that can become more and more experimental. As subsequent situations (other communities, other associations) are planned, more factors can be identified, measured, and brought under stricter control. Further, the prototype may draw attention to the importance of factors that have been previously underestimated, in this way suggesting lines of inquiry for future laboratory research.

Incorporating Computer Simulation

Computer simulation provides a spectacular addition to the available means of improving our mastery of complex situations. As yet, however, the technique of incorporating computer simulation is in an early phase of development.

It is unnecessary to rehearse at length the advantages that may be obtained by skillful mastery of the computer, or the disadvantages that have in fact accompanied many attempted applications. The new instrument has greatly sharpened the issues involved in devising a program that mediates between the verbal requirements of theory and the description of concrete situations. The model is a version of theory that makes a provisional interpretation of theory by selecting terms, definitions, rules of combination, and specific indicators or indices. The question is always open concerning the satisfactoriness of the model as a transcription of the theory, or as suitably specified to bring out the significant features of the concrete circumstances to which it is applied.

The speed of the computer has emphasized the gap that previously existed between data, analysis, and proposed policy alternatives. If the chosen indicators are to be kept up-to-date, it is necessary to plan ahead for the making of observations, and to keep alive the question of whether the indicators used in the past can be expected to have the same meaning (i.e., the same relationship to the categories for which they stand). A continuing feedback renders it feasible to make overlapping runs of new and old indicators for the purpose of evaluating the degree to which they can be substituted for one another.

Every problem-solving task can be expedited, whether it is a question of assessing policy options, the stability of trends and conditions, the clarity of goal values, or the plausibility of developmental constructs. Power relations are redefined for the benefit of computer programmers and interpreters.

The problems that arise in incorporating this new instrument can be fruitfully considered by focusing on experience to date in reference to theories and policies of political development. The political motives for many programs designed to assist development were closely related to the Cold War between the United States and the USSR. The expectation on the American side was that the introduction of new technologies of production would produce new middle classes whose political orientation at home and abroad would be toward popular government of a form that would approximate the familiar institutions of Western Europe, such as parliaments, competitive political parties, free press, and effective guarantees on behalf of individual and minority rights. It was further assumed that this sequence of changes could occur with little instability at home and hence with increasing security in the world arena as a whole.

Thanks to the availability of the economics profession and to the political popularity of slogans referring to economic development, the earliest policies were thought about and almost exclusively phrased in economic terms. It has become increasing clear that economic phenomena are interconnected with the total value-institution context in which they occur. Hence the limitations of narrowly economic models for the guidance of decision have become more evident. Economists have been enlarging the scope of their models to include more of the social process, whether they continue to employ economic terminology or not. Social scientists other than economists are making their voices heard, and are now seeking to devise computer programs that comprehensively characterize the interplay of economic, political, and all other principal features of a developing society.

At present there is much confusion and uncertainty about the most effective way to adapt existing intellectual tools and procedures to the scientific and policy tasks connected with such a fundamental field as political development. For the moment it is sufficient to distinguish three strategies presently at the disposal of policy scientists who explore or guide political evolution in national or urban settings. Brunner and Brewer, for example, observe that the phenomenon is systematically investigated by two principal methods, to which they propose to add a third. The first can be called *correlational,* the second *formal deductive,* the third *computer modeling.* The name of the computer is introduced to emphasize that when the machine is contextually yet selectively programmed it can assist the policy analyst to accomplish the continuing appraisal and reorientation functions required by his fundamental role.

Great reliance has been put on the use of statistical correlation as a means of validating propositions formulated by political and social scientists. These follow the usual practice of comparing two variables or variable clusters across national boundaries. The result is to weaken the relevancy of the results for science or policy, since the contextual significance of national entities is greatly blurred. Brunner and Brewer have demonstrated in detail how correlational procedures are often misapplied. The proper role of correlation is exploratory, *not* validating.

The second strategy or formal deduction when in expert hands is distinguished by syntactic elegance. It is able to show in systematic detail the consequences of a set of initial rules that define the interplay among the subsystems of a formally inclusive whole. The objection to giving top priority to this approach is that it is diversionary. It diverts the accomplished mathematical modelmaker toward aesthetically satisfying results. Such an approach is indeed appropriate where the data are abundant and the theoretical system is well rooted in a critical tradition. At present these requirements are not met in studies of political evolution, and efforts at excessive formalism introduce unnecessary distortions in the resulting model.

The use of a methodology adapted to partially systematized theory, scattered data, and intense demands for guidance calls for a computer technique that emphasizes the arrow of time, and the opportunity to engage in a continuing process of model improvement as data become available, and as new policy alternatives pose new questions. Computer modeling lends itself to the intensive, forward-looking study of the predispositions distributed in a given social context.

Participant Observation and Other Standpoints

The discussion in this chapter has given prominence to some of the tools by which the intellectual responsibility of the policy sciences can be at least partially fulfilled. Although the techniques dealt with are not isolated from the analysis of decision processes, and may be included at some phases, they do not entirely depend on full participation by the scientific observer in such a process at a given moment. It is impossible to obtain many of the data required for a contextual map without being President; but many relevant constructs, for instance, do not depend on the messages transmitted in the latest diplomatic pouch. Prototyping can be carried on without entering fully into the power arena of the nation state.

Nevertheless, it is clear that the policy sciences cannot reach their potential for either analysis or influence unless policy scientists are able to act as participant observers, either of themselves in important positions, or of others who are willing to be observed in action. Many questions immediately arise that relate to the role and identity of the policy science profession, and these will be considered in chapter 7.

At the moment we are calling attention to the spectrum of relationships that define the position of the scientific observer in reference to his field of observation. In addition to performing a conventional role in a given arena, a *participant observer* is recognized to have theoretical interests. One type is exemplified by the anthropologist who lives in a society remote from his own culture, and who enters rather fully into the ordinary activities of life. The natives may almost lose sight of the fact that he is going to describe them to strangers. When he is successful in defining his role, the scientific *interviewer* is also perceived as a data gatherer for scientific purposes. The interviewer presumably influences the behavior of others. Hence he and the participant observer face the technical problem of understanding the impact of themselves as potential sources of distortion.

We define a *spectator* as an observer who can describe what is going on without sharing awareness of his identity or purpose with those who are in his field of observation. The member of a crowd at the assassination of a political figure is sunk in the anonymity of the whole. The spectator is able to use his eyes, his microsize camera, and his microsize machine to record the scene. The spectator may plant secret microphones and photographing equipment in rooms where the cabinet meets, or where top executives consult with subordinates, or at clubs, bars, and restaurants which they patronize, or in living quarters.

When the records available to the scientific observer are unaffected by his presence, we refer to the standpoint of the *collector*. When past decisions are under study, and the investigator has had no contact with the participant, the situation is typical of the historian's relation to a remote event.

The available repertory of the social sciences include the technique of data gathering from several standpoints. The policy sciences rely on such established methods, and plan to extend and adapt them to many professional purposes for which they were not originally designed.

CHAPTER 5

Professional Services: The Ordinary Policy Process

Introduction

Policy scientists operate professionally in widening circles of clients, colleagues, and community. As the role of a policy scientist is better understood, the clients will entertain realistic expectations when they turn to him for professional services, particularly in connection with the planning and appraisal phases of decision. Since governmental and private organizations often fail to examine the policy process as a whole, it may not be perceived that in many instances disappointing outcomes are the result of poorly designed and mal-coordinated structures. Instead of recognizing a structural source, the trouble may be attributed to irrational opposition or an accelerating rate of change. The established routine of the policy process may discourage the anticipation of problems, and prevent the mobilization of the motives and knowledge necessary to act with speed and realism.

The Range of Clients

Policy scientists can be of assistance to those who are responsible for final decision by examining how well or poorly the policy process is operating, and by guiding attention to the effective and formal factors responsible for results. This is *policy appraisal* of the ordinary flow of decision.

Closely linked, though distinguishable from his operation, is *impact appraisal,* whose task is to deal with the effect of organization on social process. Neither policy appraisal nor impact analysis can be "completed" without the other. It is, however, easier to examine internal events and to arrive at a provisional judgment than to assess the entire social and natural environment.

A third form of appraisal is sufficiently important to be isolated for special consideration. This is *constitutive appraisal,* which examines the decision process in order to discover any significant changes that have taken place in the power position of the individuals, groups, perspectives, or operations involved. The question is whether fluctuations in power have stayed within the cyclical limits characteristic of the context, or whether they have become partially stabilized as structural changes. In the latter case the innovations are "reformist" or "revolutionary," "counterreformist" or "counterrevolutionary." The appraisal also distinguishes between *control* and *authority*, the former referring to effective and the latter to formal power.

Policy scientists are appropriately involved in *ordinary policy planning,* which is part of the intelligence function and operates within the framework of an established system of authority and control. Ordinary policy planning adapts structures and functions to the modest changes compatible with established doctrines, formulas, and miranda. Ordinary planning mobilizes the knowledge pertinent to a specific set of problems relating to wealth, well-being, and other nonpower components of public order, and endeavors to devise creative solutions to these problems. The policy science approach, with its emphasis on contextuality, fades into everyday improvisation if little time or tolerance is available to conduct the inquiries required by a thorough planning operation.

Impact planning is inseparable from any policy operation that looks beyond the internal context of decision. Totally opportunistic improvisation gives no opportunity for the kind of reality testing in advance that is called for by a policy science approach. An example of impact planning is the development of long-range programs to transform the social structure of a nation state by mobilizing the demands, expectations, and identifications necessary to weaken an ascendant landlord class and to substitute an educated professional and entrepreneurial middle class. Or, less drastically, an example is a program to decentralize both industrial and scientific facilities as a means of reducing the vulnerability of a nation to outside assault or to internal conflict along class or regional lines.

Constitutive planning is constitutional planning of the basic allocations of authority and control in a body politic. We do not use the term *constitutional* as the principal category, in view of its misleading legalistic connotations. A constitution is often assumed to be a written charter, or a set of "once and for all" arrangements. While it is true that constitutional conventions may draft an authoritative document, constitutive planning is not limited to such occasions, nor is it necessarily much concerned with a single written instrument. For instance, it may include campaigns to arouse political participation among the inert, the self-doubting, or the alienated. The peasants and the small farmers, the pupils and students, the women and the pariah castes, the small stockholders and the blue-collar workers, and the run-of-the-mill architects and engineers are among the groups whose activism depends on attaining more self-confident participation in the power processes of society.

Professional assistance by policy scientists is not limited to the planning and appraisal of *aggregate* processes at the national, transnational, or subnational level. Each *specialized* decision structure has an internal policy process, and therefore needs to give comprehensive and realistic consideration to its internal and external effectiveness.

Questions about the future are the distinctive province of the *intelligence* structures. Besides appraising the effectiveness with which the function is carried on, policy scientists can supplement the regular staff and make substantive contributions to the planning of public policy in major areas. Such a supplementary role is especially helpful when the permanent planning staff is small, staff expansion is difficult, and a problem is novel and perhaps temporary. A community may face a sudden temporary increase in population as a result of large construction projects in the vicinity (such as dam building). Or a recently recognized source of soil, water, or air pollution may require urgent attention.

Policy analysts assist in defining goals, imagining alternative courses of action, and evaluating short- and long-range costs and gains. Sometimes the principal task is to locate unusual sources of knowledge and to find personnel best able to cope with a problem.

While *promotional* activities are familiar features of official and unofficial life, policy failures in this sector are common. Public relations is a relatively recent occupation whose members aspire to professional status, and whose schools are often moving toward a policy science approach. A sound public relations professional insists on conducting investigations to discover whether a valid role can be found for a client organization or project. Often the key question is under what circumstances this or a similar organization can obtain continuing support from the social environment. The emphasis is on strategies that affect the future experience of the relevant groups. If continuing support is to be forthcoming, the focus of attention of the members of a group must include direct and communicated experience with the operation in question; further, these exposures must arouse and realize expectations of net value advantage.

The *prescribing* structures in the decision process are potential clients of policy science professionals. In contemporary popular government the legislative bodies are often alarmed by the ease with which executive bureaucracies concentrate effective power in their own hands. Whether civilian or military, the bureaucracies tend to monopolize the factual information on which the evaluation of legislative proposals depends. Besides losing control of intelligence functions, legislative bodies often recognize that promotional activities have slipped into executive hands, especially when they are faced by coalitions between administrative agencies and private interest groups. It is also true that many of the defensive tactics adopted by legislatures have backfired. A frequent example is provided by ill-considered and overdetailed interference with welfare or fiscal measures. The public impression that legislatures are an ineffective organ of government is heightened by the examples of corruption that occasionally come to general notice. It is no wonder that many legislative bodies are searching for staff and advisory assistance in order to obtain sufficient access to scientific knowledge to defend their power position in the decision process.

A highly strategic place for policy analysts to play a useful role is in structures specialized to *invocation*. Official administrators are aware of the usual disparities that separate authoritatively prescribed goals of legislation from the dollars appropriated to give them effect. Policy analysis searches for the optimum suballocation of scarce resources.

The *applying* function, which is so closely connected with invocation, typically operates in a narrowing context of choice. It continues to depend on suballocating strategies.

The decision to *terminate* is made by legislators or other authorities authorized by official prescription to put an end to an established arrangement. If claims for compensation (or some equivalent service) are to be evaluated and met, alternative programs of resource allocation must be weighed in the context of total policy.

The Problem of Trust

Trend studies indicate that while many organizations are aware of the importance of examining and supplementing their policy processes, they are not always prepared to utilize competent assistance. Experience confirms the point that the *advisory relationship is most effective when decisionmakers are willing to allow themselves and their operation to be fully examined, and to receive, as well as to make, candid disclosure.*

Men of great professional ability are often engaged by governmental and private organizations to no avail, largely because influential decisionmakers have no desire to hear the truth or are too distrustful to allow competent people to find out enough truth to be genuinely helpful.

Why do influential decisionmakers often deprive themselves of what they profess to want? A pervasive factor is socialization in a rivalrous culture. Persons reared in a *rivalrous culture learn distrust—of others and of themselves*. More particularly, the pursuit and exercise of power becomes an exercise in selective distrust. Let us briefly explore these propositions.

To be brought up in a rivalrous society is to be exposed to much deceit, false friendship, and malice. These are "real" experiences in the social environment, and anyone who succeeds in maturing learns to cope with deprivations of the kind. He learns not to disclose himself to others until it is clear that disclosure is safe, since common interests—including friendship and canons of decency—are shared. He also learns when dealing with others to use deceit, false friendship, and malice in varying degree.

These moral failings are so widely distributed in time and place that they are embedded in images of human nature as totally or partly evil. In some civilizations deception is more fully accepted and institutionalized than in others. In American society, for example, we have taught one another to expect to use, or to be the target of, a great deal of lying, especially in the market and in political arenas. Salesmen and candidates simulate friendship with us and with one another. In world politics it must be taken for granted that the expectation of violence often renders it necessary for presidents, secretaries of state, and other responsible officials to deceive and double-cross one another in the practice of diplomacy and propaganda.

By the time any of us have learned to survive in politics or business, for example, we have acquired an external facade that can be manipulated for purposes of partial deception. At the same time the successful person has learned that some men are trustworthy—if not absolutely, at least sufficiently for collegial or even friendly purposes. If the individual has not learned *selective trust as well as selective distrust he is likely to fail* and to belong in the category of the mentally ill. In extreme cases, mental illness is not difficult to detect, as when a man wraps himself in paranoid delusions and imagines that his partners or his relatives are putting poison in his martinis or manipulating his brain with an electromagnet from the top of the Empire State building. The complexities of life are complicated by an occasional news account of a court case in which the martinis were in fact poisoned and a physical therapist weakened the victim with the aid of an x-ray machine.

Influential and experienced men do not easily give full confidence. Fortunately, many decision processes can be usefully analyzed with minimum penetration into, or disclosure of, zones of privacy. Moreover, a policy analyst is often able to function at an optimum level if he maintains a degree of personal distance, and does not become so involved with a client that he subtly acquires his slant on affairs.

The decisionmaker who becomes a client of a policy analyst is well-advised to *respect the independence of the analyst, and to demonstrate his own willingness to "take" it,* even if the results are disconcerting or the recommendations, at first glance, are unwelcome.

The Problem of Complementary Interests

In common with all professionally trained persons the policy scientist has a problem in relating himself to a prospective or accepted client. The problem is complementarity. What are the client's valid objectives? How compatible are these objectives with those of the policy scientist himself?

The answer to the first question calls for a tactful and realistic exploration of the *potential client's position in the relevant decision and social processes.* In the course of a preliminary inquiry the problem is to discover who the actual client is, what he wants, whether he can get it, and what the consequences are.

An experienced legal counselor knows that it is not always easy to learn the true identity of a corporate client whose interests he is asked to represent. The nominal listings are readily at hand, but relays of brokers, attorneys, and other agents may mask a foreign government.

The initial conversations with a prospective client are crucial on both sides. A physician, in particular, is accustomed to listen attentively to a prospective patient, who typically begins by detailing his symptoms. He may ask the physician to give him a particular treatment (e.g., prescribe a certain drug). The sound practitioner is too conscious of his special knowledge and obligations to the client to take orders from him. Even without exhaustive research the physician may refuse drugs and propose something else. Similarly a lawyer may discover that the legal action demanded by a client is a mere spite action, likely to be dismissed by the courts.

The policy scientist's problem is to *assist the client to perceive his valid interests.* Perhaps the client is the temporary victim of supersalesmanship or wishful fantasy, and has acquired an exaggerated image of the consultant's instant omniscience as a "master of planning by computer." Or he may be sold on the problem-solving efficacy of "brainstorming." Under these circumstances the problem is to debunk unwise diagnoses and solutions without discrediting the kernel of truth in various policy approaches.

Common sense and formal analysis are at one in providing the policy scientist with a fundamental principle for dealing with clients. *A client will not consult or continue to use a policy advisor unless he expects to be better off than he would be by not doing so.* In theoretical terms this is implied by the maximization postulate. Since expectations are presumably affected by realizations, expectations of future benefit must be at least partly confirmed by experience. Therefore, the advisor must provide for a *stream of partial realizations without waiting indefinitely.*

It is clear that the policy scientist who desires an opportunity to serve a client must find ways of affecting the client's cognitive map. *The means by which the client's perspectives can be affected must entail a cost that is acceptable to the adviser.*

A key question is, *What value demands of the client* are sufficiently relevant to the problem at hand to be affected by *expectations?* A reply can be given when it is clear which *identities* are involved. If the client is chairman of a planning commission, is he determined to devote his life to reconstructing the city? Is he a professional planner who expects to be invited to bigger cities or to a top national post and who is therefore disposed to perceive the immediate task as a step up the career ladder? Is the client a top political figure who eventually aspires to be elected governor or senator, and who desires to cultivate the support of liberal journalists, commentators, academic figures, politicians and contributors? Or is he disinterested in liberals and is instead responsive to businessmen active in real estate, construction, banking and finance, commerce (department stores, supermarkets), and utilities (i.e., electricity, coal, oil, gas, rails, telephones, railways, aviation)? Or is he sensitive to the sentiments of construction workers, veterans, and locally dominant ethnic and religious groups?

If the social process map is systematically utilized as a reminder of the entire context of values and institutions, it sharpens the image of a client's identity, value demands, and expectations. Such an image is a step toward clarifying the criteria that will affect the future relations of advisor and client.

Among the internal adjustments required by the policy scientist in relation to the client is *willingness to stay out of the spotlight.* One of the oldest axioms among professional civil servants and private advisors insists on a "passion for anonymity." After all, it is the client who must take the rap if his decision is wrong, including his choice of advisors and other assistants. It is the client who is to be built up, not the policy scientist. The latter must have enough confidence in himself and his role to understand that word-of-mouth publicity will play the most definitive part in his career, and that an attempt to steal the show will backfire.

Experience underlines another item of realistic folklore. The advisory operation must have the reputation for, and the fact of, *top-level support*. As implied above, the significant power figures should know as far as possible what is going on and what they can expect to get out of it—and they should still want it. This implies that a policy scientist should "have access" to and maintain definite liaison arrangements.

Also essential to the undertaking is *an inside support staff* that is thoroughly conversant with the routines of administration, including the relevant personnel and the hidden as well as public assets in the organization. The essential point is to work *with* and not against those who have the skill necessary to turn top-level authority into the effective control necessary to get the job done. The policy analyst takes it for granted that he works as part of a team (a coalition) of actual and potential allies, with whom he identifies, compares maps (large or small), and defines value objectives (general or particular). The career civil servant is not necessarily a policy scientist, although it is a great advantage if he has such training and experience. Nor is the top official or political figure necessarily a policy scientist. In the rush of things top leaders have little time for most matters; hence they need the assistance of those who take a longer view of the situation. "In-house" planners and appraisers are similarly in need of outside professional assistance. If they have had a policy science background or have acquired such a viewpoint the hard way, they are the first to recognize the advantages of independent advisors. They can often utilize the outsider as a conveyor belt for ideas that gain resonance when they are relayed over a loudspeaker whose unfamiliarity breeds upper echelon attention. If the "in-house" specialists are allowed to behave as true professionals, they are willing to encourage and to live with recommendations with which they are not entirely in accord.

All principal-client relations cannot be expected to be sweetness and light. They can, however, be creative and tolerable. And as the whole approach is more adequately articulated and institutionalized, the implications for continuing innovation will be clear in the adjustment of public order institutions to long-range goals.

The relationship between client and principal is a duality in which perceptions of common interest shade off in all directions. Moreover, while individuals are especially important for short-range collaboration, large operational entities impose severe constraints on the whole process. Where individual and institutional factors combine to ease the path for the policy scientist, the results may be spectacular. Over short periods, at least, nothing succeeds like visible success. At the same time *success must be kept suspect,* particularly when all seems to be going well.

One cautionary proposition is that *short-range success is often the parent of long-range failure.* This formulation is no paradox to be dismissed as a plausible though idle literary conceit. It emphasizes a built-in source of potential failure in individual lives and organizations. As the maximization postulate implies, we tend to repeat the strategies whose pay-offs—in all value categories—are perceived as indulgant, not deprivational. Basic psychological mechanisms tend to stabilize, even to rigidify, our perceptions of the self in relation to the environment. The mechanism of generalization operates by suffusing the entire picture of reality with the sunlight of success or the darkness of defeat. In the case of a successful outcome the positive experience generalizes backward and confers a positive aura on the strategies employed at the preoutcome phases of decision. The cues that were part of the perspectives used to identify a situation to which the strategies were appropriately applied are similarly affected. Cumulative success tends to narrow the context that is allowed to emerge at the focus of attention.

These narrowing images of the "self-in-situation" are hidden dangers. Therefore policy scientists are well advised on occasion to play the devil's advocate with themselves and a client in the hope of weakening the standardization of success, since it is likely to become a standardization of error in dealing with unrecognized changes in the situation. The man of caution is likely to be confirmed in his caution, and to win respect for his good judgment. So long as the situation remains substantially the same, no damage is done. If, however, structural transformations are under way, the chances of failure are increased by cautious rigidity. If the policy process gives power and respect to the "bureaucratic mentality," the decisionmakers with a long record of success prepare the organization for eventual crisis, even failure.

The repetitive tendency is strongly sustained by the flow of lesser decisions that follow in the wake of a successful crisis and adjustment. At the macro-level the rigidifying consequences of success are exhibited in the often-noted tendency of victorious armies to prepare for the war they had won, rather than for the war that came. It was the defeated Germans after World War I who took the lead in perceiving the significance of tanks and bombing planes. It is the rural-based revolutionaries of Red China, not the urban and factory-based legatees of 1917, who dominate the strategy of recent times.

The Criteria of Policy

A fundamental aim of the policy scientist in dealing with a client organization is to bring about an improved capability in the formation and execution of policy. If this capability is to be achieved, the most significant figures in the operation must become personally involved. A crucial step is the formulation of relevant criteria. It is essential to locate decisionmakers of sufficient weight, commitment, and breadth of view to become direct participants rather than participants by hired and delegated proxy.

In a world of great scope and complexity it is more than ever important for responsible decisionmakers to subject themselves to the discipline required to keep in touch with reality and especially with alternative versions of the truth. The problem is more acute as the computer is institutionalized. A new layer of skilled personnel is emerging in large organizations, whose job is to read and select from the swollen stream of information provided by the computer network. Unless top policy participants discover means of going behind the summaries, they will be unable to master the flood and to use modern instruments in aid of realism and creativity. By keeping a comprehensive conceptual map at the focus of their attention, they can define objectives and select criteria of performance that guide attention to significant features of the operations in which they are involved. They are able to probe seeming inconsistencies, contradictions, deceptions, and mistakes, and to bring their judgment to bear at strategic points.

In the following pages a relatively systematic summary is provided of the great range of criteria that are potentially pertinent to every policy structure and function. It should not be assumed that the summary is to be employed in pedantic fashion to introduce decisionmakers to the problem of choosing the criteria salient to their organization. Rather, the analysis is a working sketch of possibilities. The analysis can be utilized by policy analysts themselves for whatever advantages it may have as a reminder of ramifying complexity.

Initial discussions are most effective when they begin with the viewpoints and vocabulary with which the participants are comfortable. As discussions continue, they grow in depth and spread, and require partial systematization. In this evolutionary fashion every group is able to develop its distinctive version of the social context and the decision process. The policy analyst operates with his own comprehensive map in the background, not for the purpose of imposing its terms or meanings on the group, but rather as an instrument of equivalence. The challenge is to encourage the discovery of equivalencies for his own cognitive map, and to use whatever words (or word equivalents) will allow an equally comprehensive map to appear in the group situation.

It often happens that previous familiarity with the system of thought and talk outlined here enables a group to function within the concepts and terms of the system. Presumably this may happen more often in the next few years. However, it is not essential. In principle all comprehensive conceptual maps of the social and policy process are equivalent to one another. For instance, they employ terms for *whole* or *part* (such as *social process* for the former, and a specific category like *power* or *respect* for a component part).

The problem of moving from a *concept* to an *index* or *indicator* is always present. The choice of indices depends on the procedures of observation and recording that the group has in view. For example, one of the criteria commonly proposed for the intelligence function is a balanced presentation of conflicting versions of fact or of normative recommendations. If this criterion is to be applied to the mass media, it is necessary to analyze the content of news and editorial presentations. The analyst must decide the minimum frequency that a given version of fact or a normative proposal must receive (in radio-television programs or the press) before it is eligible for inclusion as one of the presentations to be balanced. How are balances to be defined (e.g., 50–50, 60–40)?

The present analysis begins by considering each decision outcome or structure separately. It is possible to formulate policy criteria in such a way that they clearly apply to each component and also to the whole decision process. However, each of the seven outcome functions in our theoretical model gives prominence to some criteria above others, and we bring these differences into the open by proceeding from outcome to outcome.

When criteria have been formulated for the seven outcomes separately, we identify additional criteria that obviously apply to each structure or function independently or in the aggregate. A brief comment or example is given for the sake of clarity.

Criteria for the Intelligence Function

1.1 *Dependability*

Statements of fact that are made available to other members of the decision process are dependable; and if there is doubt, an indication is given of probable credibility.

The presence or absence of guides to credibility can be ascertained by analyzing the content of written or recorded reports.

1.11 Sources for descriptive statements are representative of the best available.

Analyses may show the qualifications of the experts (or publications) quoted. Knowledgeable panels may evaluate the qualifications as first-rate, acceptable, doubtful, or very questionable.

1.12 The sources are motivated to supply realistic statements when assessed at the conscious or unconscious level.

Analyses may include classification according to loyalty (identification) where relevant.

1.13 Competence is mobilized and applied in pertinent situations. The question is whether there was an opportunity to use appropriate methods and whether they were actually employed.

The observational opportunity can be rated where it counts, such as physical presence at the scene of a negotiation.

1.14 Statements are accurately transmitted.

Content analysis can be used to follow the fate of assertions from the original source through subsequent transmissions and editing.

1.15 Recipients are able and willing to *acknowledge* the credibility of realistic statements. This criterion refers to the success of the intelligence function in obtaining the confidence of others.

Confidential or open surveys are helpful on this point.

1.2 *Comprehensiveness*

The output includes the messages pertinent to all problems in the decision process.

For instance, have trend, condition, and projection data about group attitudes been reported or neglected?

1.21 The output is inclusive in terms of the goals sought in the total process.

Have the statutes, treaties, or other relevant authoritative assertions been explored, analyzed, and utilized?

1.22 It is inclusive in regard to trends, revealing both favorable and unfavorable changes.

1.23 It is inclusive of pertinent conditioning factors. Major explanations are included, and controversial assertions are explicitly reported.

1.24 Projections are inclusive of the general goals and particular objectives sought.

1.25 The inclusive analysis of policy alternatives calls for benefit, cost, and risk of each.

1.3 *Selectivity*

1.31 Outputs are related to perceived problems. What proportion of outputs have been at the initiative of users or of persons within the service?

1.32 Priorities are indicated when a problem is imminent and important according to the values at stake.

1.4 *Creativity*

1.41 New and realistic objectives and strategies are compared with older or less realistic alternatives.

Panels of experts selected according to explicit criteria can be utilized to classify output according to novelty and realism.

1.5 *Openness*

1.51 This criterion mobilizes the demand by participants for intelligence pertinent to both immediate and long-range problems.

A summary can be made of liaison and other efforts to reach public or particular groups and individuals.

1.52 Cooperation in obtaining intelligence is elicited.

Indicators are needed of the amount and importance of information volunteered or resulting from an agreement.

1.53 The output is closed to unauthorized persons and organizations for appropriate periods. Restrictions on dissemination are reasonable when lawful goals would be comprised, or when avoidable deprivations are imposed on third parties.

Interviews and content analysis of media can indicate the flow of unauthorized information.

Criteria for the Promotional Function

2.1 *Rationality*

Promotional activities bring to the focus of attention of decisionmakers proposals and justifications with sufficient fullness to permit judgments of priority to be made.

What information has been made available about the probability of value indulgences or deprivation in the immediate or longer-range future?

2.11 Relevant selections are made from the stock of available intelligence.

In selected recent situations what was over- or underemphasized in party, interest group, or other promotional group communications?

2.2 *Integrativeness*

Initial uncertainties and conflicts are resolved by programs that mobilize general support.

2.21 A truly integrative solution is one that the parties do not perceive as a patchwork of compromises in which wins and losses can be identified. For instance, competing programs for antipollution may be fused in a larger environmental defense proposal.

What formulations (by value-institution category) received approval at what stage of controversy? What demands have not generated a workable compromise or a genuine redefinition and discovery of common interest?

2.22 When competing political parties, pressure associations, or coalitions cannot integrate, they can bipolarize issues in yes or no, either-or forms that permit public opinion to clarify action alternatives.

What demands will arrive at what phase in the immediate and longer future?

2.23 Promotional activities do not arouse such intensity of involvement that coercive acts occur.

The frequency, location, and factors contributing to peaceful demonstrations, lobbying, etc., should be considered.

2.3 *Comprehensiveness*

All participants in the social and political process are activated with sufficient frequency to permit the formation of programs that reflect the full range of community interests.

Trends in the comprehensiveness of programs of parties, interest groups, etc., should be studied.

2.31 Initiatives are taken that probe for discontents among those who may not have sufficient confidence in their potential influence to bestir themselves to make demands. This has often been true of poverty areas.

What are the volume and the nature of initiatives obtained by interviewing or solicitation?

2.32 Promotional activities mobilize informed and outspoken judgment promptly enough to nullify propensities for enthusiastic endorsement of programs that, if adopted, would prove destructive. This criterion is not satisfactorily applicable so far as future events are concerned. However, the criterion can be applied to some recent events.

Has there been a time lag in mobilizing endorsement of programs ameliorating discontent?

2.33 Promotional activities reach and mobilize the latent demands of groups that perceive themselves as weak and neglected. The bureaucratizing tendencies of organized political party and pressure groups are counteracted. The "middle elite" elements of these organizations tend to deal with one another in preference to working actively to stimulate the rank and file. The ultimate consequence of tacit nonrepresentation in promotional activities is to create a revolutionary crisis of explosive protest.

What are the trends of nonvoting or other forms of nonparticipation, of discontent and destructive action?

Criteria for the Prescribing Function

3.1 *Stability of expectation*

The stability of expectation is established about lawfulness.

The scope and range of prescriptions whose lawfulness and enforceability are doubted by various groups should be determined, by interview with lawyers, etc.

3.11 Prescriptions for which there is general demand, and which are likely to continue to receive support, are enacted promptly.

A summary of the lag in prescription from public recommendation to enactment can be made, what are the predictions for the future?

3.12 Prescriptions are avoided, despite general demand, if support is not likely to continue. Confidence in public order is strengthened when the system is capable of "enforcing pause" and preventing destructive or unworkable programs from receiving the dignity of enactment.

What is the trend in instances of resisting "unenforceable" demands, or of giving in to them?

3.13 Prior to enactment, prescriptions are brought to the attention of groups beyond those most immediately interested. In view of the large volume of legislation required in modern bodies politic, it is important to activate particular arrangements (e.g., "notice and hearing," the broadcasting of committee hearings, the publicizing of enactments) to reach the attention of third-party groups, even though relatively small in size.

What is the trend in volume of attention in public and particular media given to various categories of prescription?

3-14. Prescriptions formulate long-range and instrumental goals. More specifically a prescription includes *(a)* norms, *(b)* contingencies, or the factual circumstances to which norms apply, and *(c)* sanctions or the indulgences and deprivations resulting from conformity or nonconformity. Assets are also provided to administer the act and to appraise the result.

The trends in comprehensiveness and adequacy of drafting (critical omissions, etc.) may be studied.

3.2 *Rationality*

Prescriptions are formulated to give effect to common, not special, interests, and to balance inclusive and exclusive interests.

An analysis can be made by expert panels of the probable interest-group consequences of the flow of formulated prescriptions in value-institution areas.

3.3 *Comprehensiveness*

Prescriptions anticipate and provide for all interactions that significantly affect common interests.

As above, expert panels may be used, in this case to focus on the range of factual contingencies foreseen or omitted.

3.31 For example, if the prescription is formulated during a high, middle, or low crisis period, the other contingencies are explicitly dealt with.

3.32 Sanctions are formulated to *deter* nonconformity by specifying the value deprivations that follow.

3.33 Sanctions are formulated to *resist* acts of nonconformity and to block the deprivations that they inflict.

3.34 Sanctions arc formulated to *rehabilitate* persons and restore damaged assets.

3.35 Sanctions are formulated to *prevent* future recurrences, while remaining in the framework of the whole system.

3.36 Sanctions are formulated to *correct* motivations and deficiencies of education that stimulate nonconformity.

3.37 Sanctions are formulated to *reconstruct* institutions in ways that encourage conformity.

Criteria for the Invoking Function

4.1 *Timeliness*

This is especially urgent when value deprivations are alleged.

The trend in lag between precipitating events, complaints, and initial action can be studied.

4.11 Justifiable complaints on the part of the impoverished are encouraged.

What is the trend in complaints by the poor on specific matters, and in subsequent action officially initiated?

4.2 *Dependability*

Discrepancies in concrete instances may occur between authorization and performance.

4.21 This calls for supplementing the facts gathered by the general intelligence agencies through independent inquiries directed to the concrete case.

What is the trend in action by category of prescription and factual context?

4.3 *Rationality*

To be responsive to the common interest is to initiate action in circumstances in harmony with the contingencies referred to in prescriptions.

What are the trends in justified or unjustified rejection or affirmative action on complaints?

4.31 Summary procedures are used in situations of imminent destruction, or in the presence of destructive acts.

The trend in summary procedures in identifiable circumstances may be studied.

4.32 Since summary procedures are especially open to abuse, preliminary inquiries are more likely to guide action with rationality and realism.

What are the trends in the use of preliminary inquiry of various depth?

4.4 *Nonprovocativeness*

Initiatives impose no more deprivations than are required (e.g., officials are nonabusive).

There may be trend sampling of the behavior of police and other officials who initiate or immediately respond to invocations.

Criteria for Application

5.1 *Rationality and realism*

The process is guided by the common interest formulated in prescriptions.

5.11 Where several steps and agencies are involved, the problem is to supervise and review performance throughout and to rectify nonconformity.

There is trend sampling of actions or failure to act at each interface where activities occur.

5.2 *Uniformity*

The process is applied without discriminatory deprivations.

A sampling is necessary according to the category of client (value position in social process).

5.21 If special interests are to be neutralized, third-party participants are mobilized. This is particularly vital for large-scale operations.

What are the trends in regulatory, supervisory, or enterprisory controversies?

Criteria for Termination

6.1 *Timeliness*

This criterion calls for prompt dealing with obsolete prescriptions and particular interests.

What is the sampled time lag in reporting and terminating?

6.2 *Dependability and comprehensiveness*

An exploration of facts and policies emphasizes both dependability and comprehensiveness.

An analysis of representative cases can be made.

6.3 *Balance*

Balances are maintained between expediting or inhibiting change.

Panels estimate the impact of policies on reluctance to initiate new business or other activities.

6.4 *Ameliorativeness*

Destructive impacts of change are minimalized.

What is the trend in disposition of cases that involve deprivation of previous value position?

6.41 No compensating arrangements are made if strong, coercive opposition to public policy is likely to continue.

What degree of recent coerciveness is attributable to policies?

6.42 Windfall advantages are expropriated.

Criteria of the Appraisal Function

7.1 *Dependability and rationality*

7.11 The policies and the criteria are agreed upon.

7.12 The data are dependable.

7.13 The explanatory analyses are relevant and explicit.

7.14 The imputations of formal responsibility are explicit.

Authoritativeness of norms of responsibility are estimated from statutes, court decisions, and other pertinent sources.

7.2 *Comprehensiveness and selectivity*

These are especially pertinent to the appraisal of total impact. Note the sampling procedures applied to various sectors in the social process model.

7.3 *Independence*

Appraisers are insulated from immediate pressures of threat or inducement, and either involve the entire context or representatives of third-party judgment.

7.31 Internal appraisers are supplemented by external appraisal.

To what degree is "in-house" personnel supplemented by independent persons or organizations?

7.4 *Continuity*

Although intermittent appraisals remobilize needed attention and support, the effects are greatest when basically continuous.

Criteria for All Functions and Structures

Among the criteria obviously appropriate to all functions and structures are *money economy* and *technical efficiency*. The wealth values that pass through a process can be described in terms of money input and output, which allows a calculation to be made of value added and cost or return per unit. The resources employed in a process can be described according to the magnitude of the materials assigned to the operations, and the magnitudes delivered as an output. Instead of salaries per capita the reference is to man-hours; instead of rent the reference is to feet of floor space; in place of cost of supplies the record is in terms of tons of cards or paper processed. Taken by itself each item is a *detail*. It is not a *datum* until it has been made pertinent to a defined criterion for the policy process. For example, the tons of paper may be described as among the "number of acceptable information bits" produced by the intelligence function, which may be an indicator of one component of the outcomes sought by intelligence.

Two other criteria are *honesty* and *reputation for honesty*. Honesty can be given a relatively simple initial definition, such as conformity to norms of financial integrity in the exercise of official responsibilities. To say that 5 percent of public funds is illicitly diverted to private income is a datum of obvious pertinence to the entire decision operation. But if the policy process is defined more restrictively to include the relatively explicit formulators and executors of public prescriptions, the revised datum might indicate that only 1 percent of the total could be attributed to dishonesty on the part of legislators and judges, for instance. The remaining 9 percent may be attributable to petty administrators, party politicians, and government suppliers. *Reputation for honesty* is an intelligible criterion that can be made operational by appropriate survey and intensive interview methods of obtaining opinions. A fascinating question is the discrepancy between the indicators of honesty obtained by the scientific appraiser and the indicators that describe the prevailing perspectives among different sectors of the community. Our assumption is that a goal of a public policy process is to deserve and also to inspire confidence in its integrity.

Further criteria of the total process refer to the *loyalty and skill of official personnel*. By loyalty is meant commitment to the overriding goals of public policy. It will be recalled that we have adopted, for purposes of this analysis, the goal of realizing human dignity in theory and practice. If a policy sciences approach were employed in a self-perpetuating caste society, it is evident that loyalty would have a drastically different content. Many skills, however, would remain the same.

Another general criterion is *complementarity and effectiveness of impact,* which means that every function is fulfilled in such a manner that it contributes to the mobilization of *immediate and continuing political support for the political system* as a whole. *It also contributes in all value-institution sectors to realizing the overriding goals of the whole polity.* Although ordinary planning and appraisal studies can be carried to a certain degree of refinement in the absence of impact analysis, the conjoining of the two is ultimately important.

Another criterion directs attention to whether a function is sufficiently developed in an aggregate decision process to be expressed through a *differentiated organ:* for instance, if intelligence or appraisal structures do not exist separately, it is improbable that the function is adequately recognized and strongly supported. In large structures a *differentiated intrastructural* organ is probably required to make sure of the independence and vigor of the operations involved.

A further criterion of general significance is *flexibility and realism in adjusting to changed circumstances.* In the absence of a major crisis (or, on the contrary, of a noncrisis period) it may be impossible to make satisfactory estimates of performance potential.

An affirmatively stated synoptic criterion for the whole system is *deliberateness and responsibility in decisionmaking and execution.* The negative circumstances are *erratic* and *impulsive* decisionmaking, or erosion of responsibility.

Table 2 is a check list of the various criteria we have mentioned. We reiterate that all criteria are pertinent to each function and structure, even though they typically receive special emphasis in connection with particular structures or functions.

Varying Levels of Analysis

The table suggests the widely ramifying criteria appropriate for ordinary policy planning or appraisal. It is important to recognize, however, that it is usually appropriate and necessary to operate with drastic simplifications. One "heroic" simplification is to restrict attention to a limited number of indicators of malfunction, since these may show where structural changes are needed.

Malfunctioning is strongly suggested by bottlenecks, such as lengthening intervals between complaints or arrests and dispositions of the matter; by costs that go up faster than the rate of monetary inflation; or by costs that

TABLE 2

Criteria of Policy Process

Component Function or Structure Criterion

	Intelligence	Promotion	Prescription	Invocation	Application	Termination	Appraisal
Dependability	x			x		x	x
Comprehensiveness	x	x	x			x	x
Selectivity	x						x
Creativity	x						
Openness	x						
Rationality & realism		x	x	x	x		x
Integrativeness	x						
Stability of expectation			x				
Timeliness				x		x	
Nonprovocativeness				x			
Uniformity					x		
Timeliness						x	
Balance						x	
Ameliorativeness						x	
Independence							x
Continuity							x

General Function or Structure

Honesty
Reputation for honesty*
Money economy
Technical efficiency
Loyalty and skill of official personnel
Complementarity and effectiveness of
    impact (in decision and social process)
Differentiated structures
Flexibility and realism in adjustment to change
Deliberateness and responsibility

* "Reputation for" should be added to every criterion where such perspectives are significant.

increase faster than in comparable communities. Either the policy process failed to anticipate conditions or made poor resource allocations.

It is often useful to run tests of prediction that summarize the performance of intelligence and especially planning agencies in order to identify (1) contingency predictions that did not come true as a result of the policy actions taken to obviate the occurrence; (2) forecasts that were contradicted by events; and (3) developments that were not anticipated.

Some of the data required for the criteria of ordinary policy appraisal belong more specifically to *impact* analysis. They are, however, of such contextual relevance that they must be included wherever possible. We referred, for instance, to the degrees of alienation and destructive opposition, which indicate the intensity with which a *political* system is supported or opposed, and serve as rough measures of the success or failure of the decision process in accumulating or failing to accumulate support. It is to be noted that the appropriate indicators utilize the three elementary components of a completed act. They refer to *symbols* (subjective events), as indicated by words and word equivalents, *deeds* (behaviors), such as fighting and killing, and *resources*, which may involve the mobilization of manpower and facilities for the army or police forces.

Impact studies also include the mustering of indicators of all the value-institution sectors other than power. In each sector the policy scientist performs a useful task in identifying panels of informed or imaginative men of knowledge whose judgment can be mobilized for intelligence and appraisal. The most economical and rapid way to initiate a comprehensive impact analysis is to use as indicators the opinions expressed by qualified panelists. However, judgment is a second-best source, and an adequate impact appraisal or planning process deals directly with the primary data and scientific explanations.

Although the computer provides a tool of great importance, we have suggested some of the limitations on its present use for policy science and professional practice. As these limitations are superseded, the comprehensive models will simulate past trends and conditions, together with probable and preferred projections of future events.

Because of its fundamental policy relevance we must give particular attention to *constitutive* appraisal and planning, which are areas where the policy sciences can be expected to perform a progressively more significant professional role.

CHAPTER 6

Professional Services: The Constitutive Policy Process

Introduction

The advisory role on a problem of allocating power has usually been played by specialists whose backgrounds, though diverse, are often in the field of public law, political science, and political philosophy. Although consultants have sometimes surmounted the limitations of a particular skill and achieved an approach that is both creative and contextual, the record is full of instances of unnecessary adherence on their part to dogmatic and narrow predispositions, whether the opportunity open to them arose at the national, transnational, or subnational level. During the period of European ascendancy it was not unusual for eminent academic figures to be invited to introduce popular government into semi-independent or newly independent countries in Asia or other continents outside Europe. The anticolonial revolutionaries of recent times have less frequently summoned an authority from the older establishment to assist in consolidating the new order. Nevertheless, policy problems connected with economic development have led to more than casual infusions of foreign advice. On the whole, in the years since World War II there has been a notable absence of preoccupation with constitution drafting. Torn by uncertainty, new leaders have temporized until expectations begin to crystallize about *who* is authorized to decide *what*. Then it may seem expedient to revive the emphasis on written documents that has so often added an element of stability to community perspectives.

The Role of Formulated Authority and Control

Policy scientists do indeed concern themselves with *formulated* statements of authority. As we have insisted, however, it is important not to confuse

98

words with *law* or *deeds* (to mention two recurring sources of confusion and error). Written words, even when impressively inscribed on parchment, or carved in stone, and celebrated as a "covenant," "compact," or "fundamental law," are *among* the indicators of law. In view of the mistakes embedded in popular usage—and often in technical literature—it may be worth reiterating that a law is *authoritative and controlling expectation about who, acting how, is justified in making enforceable decisions.* To be authoritative is to be identified as the official or agency competent to act; to be controlling is to be able to shape results. As usual, the indices of expectation are inferences from both words and deeds, and include the written words of formulated policy.

The act of bringing about the acceptance of a written text is often an important event in the evolution of a body politic. The scientist who acts as an advisor may make an important contribution to future decisionmaking by providing a model in tackling his own problems. For example, the advisor may introduce devices such as the continuing seminar.

While the text of a written document is not to be confused with the expectations current at the time of adoption, or later, it would be a mistake to assume that a document is without significance. The function of writing, or of any other method of recording a text, is to provide an authoritative frame of reference for succeeding generations. The key formulas that are made articulate in the instrument are condensed into key slogans and symbols for use in civic education, political discourse, and judicial dialectic.

The existence of an authoritative text generates an untold number of channel-to-audience situations. In this way the document enters into the culture-shaping experiences of society. *These exposure experiences become part of the culture and merge with the system of identity that ties individuals to the collective whole and provides a set of standard cues by which collective attention and action are elicited.* The terms and definitions of the document are always present as an authoritative source whose manifest content is available as a rallying point to be invoked against alleged acts of oppression by public authorities. If the document includes rhetoric about human dignity or freedom, the phrases are a perpetual source of possible protest against abuse. Written covenants are of help in stabilizing a collective frame of reference relating to all problem-solving activities. They prescribe the overriding goals and instrumental arrangements of the body politic, and spell out institutional practices that are both authoritative and controlling. The policy scientist who serves as an advisor in the formulation of a constitutional charter has an opportunity to initiate or to consolidate an institutional practice that may outlast his own and many successor generations.

Goals and Principles

If a policy scientist is to think with appropriate realism about a specific problem of allocating authority and control, he must operate with a frame of reference that fills the gaps that lie between a generalized goal model and the concrete circumstances in which power arrangements are to be established. Principles of intermediate generality are helpful when they guide the focus of attention of the problem solver back and forth between contextual aims and contextual data, and encourage the invention of institutional solutions.

The constitutive advisor *looks beyond immediate consent to long-range compliance*. It is important, for example, to take into account a fundamental point about power and the social context: *a political culture of shared power tends to strengthen tendencies toward a shared distribution of all values; conversely, wide sharing of other values than power supports the continuation of shared power*.

Clearly a guiding principle for establishing and maintaining free government is to *bring about a supporting equilibrium in which all institutions play a part*. If the problem is to foster the democratization of authority and control, the principle is: *As a preliminary to modifying the structure of formal authority in the direction of shared power, prepare the preconditions of successful operation by obtaining a substantial degree of effective control for the supporters of democracy*.

The following outline summarizes for the use of policy scientists (and thoughtful participants in a constitutive process) generalized recommendations about the objectives of a power-sharing goal. The presentation will follow the outline below, adding enough commentary to assist in amplifying its meaning.

1. The overriding goal (in brief)
2. Component objectives
   a) Effects sought in the social process
   b) Delimitation of the fields of governmental activity (in supplement to constitutive): (1) enterprisory, (2) regulative, (3) supervisory, (4) sanctioning-corrective
   c) The phases and components of the decision process
      (1) Phases: intelligence, promotion, prescription, invocation, application, appraisal, termination
      (2) Components (of each phase): participants, perspectives, arenas, base values, strategies, outcomes, effects

The outline can be rephrased in ways that formulate the criteria to be employed by a policy scientist who is assisting a decisionmaker or a decision-making group to appraise rather than to plan a decision process in constitutive terms. Since the statements made in the preceding chapter were manipulatively rather than contemplatively formulated, the present chapter is used to suggest how a more dynamic or "planning" approach can be made explicit.

As a means of exemplifying the translation problem, consider the first statement made in the presentation below about the overriding goal. For purposes of appraisal the statement must be reverbalized: "To appraise the degree to which a structure of authority and control is functioning that exemplifies and contributes to the realization of the public order of human dignity on the widest possible scale."

In the discussion of ordinary policy appraisal and planning we emphasized the interconnections with impact analysis. The parallel point applies to constitutive planning and appraisal and to impact analysis. Constitutive appraisal is designed for those who want to improve the self-observational procedures of the world (1) by discerning the impact of a given set of *constitutive predispositions* on the *subsequent constitutive responses* of a body politic when exposed to various *environmental circumstances,* and (2) by estimating the impact of *constitutive predispositions and responses* on the *fundamental institutions of values other than power,* on *the levels of value shaping,* and on *the distribution pattern of value sharing.* Trend and conditioning operations of both kinds are pertinent to the remaining intellectual tasks of goal clarification, projections of the future, and the discovery of policy alternatives. The planning rhetoric can be modified for the appraisal function in decision.

1. The overriding goal (in brief)
   To establish and maintain a structure of authority and control that exemplifies and contributes to the realization of the public order of human dignity on the widest possible scale
2a. Effects sought in the social process
   (1) To achieve under all circumstances at least a minimum public order in which coercive relations are kept at a low level, and in which whatever coercions are used are monopolized by responsible public authorities, and employed to protect the practice of persuasion in human affairs
   (2) To prepare the way for, and to consolidate, an optimum public order in which the institutions of society are voluntarily adapted

to obtaining maximum participation for all in the shaping and sharing of social values

(3) To consolidate a power process that sacrifices the values of human dignity as little as possible and is perceived throughout society as living up to this requirement

For example, power is exercised in the common interest; participants are treated with impartiality (equal basic respect); operations are conducted at a high level of competence; public affairs are not anxiety producing; interpersonal relations are humane (empathic); participants take a responsible view of their roles and search for an enlightened map of the context; and adequate facilities are available to the decisionmakers of the community for the performance of their tasks.

(4) To obtain uniformity of expectation at a given time in regard to the structure and function of authority and control

(5) To obtain stability of expectation through time in regard to the structure and function of authority and control

(6) To clarify and sustain value demands compatible with the recommended overriding goal of the system of public order

(7) To support effective identification of individuals with the whole community

(8) To foster the employment of operational techniques within the decision process and throughout society that harmonize with the fundamental objective

(9) To develop and safeguard a relationship between the myth of power and the other value myths in society that harmonize with the basic goal

(10) To achieve and stabilize an interrelationship between indulgences and deprivations, in terms of power and of other values, that sustains the expectation that the public order of human dignity is, on the whole, advantageous

(11) To foster patterns of personality that support the decision process and the system of public order consonant with the basic goal

2*b*. Delimitation of the role of government in society

(1) To achieve a balance of activities in the decision process and in society that serves public order interests. Public order interests are best effectuated by procedures with severe sanctions at their disposal. (A civic order interest is a public interest adequately realized by procedures with mild sanctions at their disposal.)

(2) To provide for the carrying out of enterprisory activities when alternative channels are likely to result in coercive relationships, or value gains at relatively high cost

(3) To engage in regulatory activities if required to limit permissible inequality in value patterns, either by establishing and maintaining upper or lower limits ("ceilings," "floors")

(4) To make supervisory services available at the request of private parties when failure to provide the service endangers the preferred system of public order

(5) To adapt sanctioning policies to the objectives of deterrence, restoration, rehabilitation, prevention, and reconstruction

   (a) The main objective of deterrence is to lead an incipient norm violator to regard the proposed violation as likely to result in a net value deprivation.

   (b) The principal objective of restoration is to bring a violation to an end and to return as far as possible to the original state of affairs.

   (c) The main purpose of rehabilitation is to undo, or to compensate for, the deprivations resulting from a norm violation.

   (d) The chief objective of prevention is to diminish the probability of norm violation by taking measures to reduce the likelihood of provocative situations.

   (e) The main objective of reconstruction is to transform the basic patterns of the social situation as a means of reducing the probability of norm violation.

(6) To distinguish between ordinary sanction problems and corrective problems. The latter involve norm deviants who are "nonresponsible," that is, who are unable by reason of defect or insufficient opportunity to acquire the norms of public order.

2c. Objectives relating to the phases and components of the decision process

   (1) To achieve and maintain a decision process whose phases operate as a dynamic equilibrium in support of the preferred goals of the system of public order (phases: intelligence, promotion, prescription, invocation, application, appraisal, termination)

   (2) To bring into being and to maintain for each phase of the decision process a structure that functions according to the fundamental aim of the system

(3) To foster an adjustment among the components of each decision structure that is contributory to the total objective (participants, perspectives, arenas, base values, strategies, outcomes, effects)

(4) To foster the selection of capable participants in each structure that is specialized to each phase of the decision process

(5) To foster the selection of participants in each structure whose perspectives are appropriate to the task, that is, whose beliefs, loyalties, and faiths are in harmony with the objectives of decision

(6) To exclude from full participation those who are committed to competing systems of public order, and who engage in activities that endanger the established system by the use of coercive methods

(7) To adapt organized arenas to the effective structure of value-shaping and value-sharing activities in the social process by adjusting inclusive and exclusive interests to one another. (Inclusive interests are value consequences important to all participants; exclusive interests are value consequences which, though common interests, are highly localized in significant value consequences.) The degree of authoritative participation in an arena is to be adapted postively to the degree of inclusive or exclusive interest at stake. Hence the arenas are to be opened to all who are affected according to the degree of involvement, and flexibly adapted to change.

(8) To provide authority as a base value proportionate to the scope, range, and domain of the function to be performed by the particular participant in an arena or by the aggregate of participants, and adequate to the acquisition of other base values required

(9) To support strategies of minimum resort to coercion and of positive emphasis upon persuasion in employing communicative, diplomatic, economic, and military instrumentalities of policy

(10) To maintain a flow of outcomes that, when deviations from basic goal are necessary to maintain the public order system, demonstrates that the deviation is temporary, and acts continually to overcome discrepancies between goal and fact

(11) To employ coercion at the outcome phase of decision wherever necessary to nullify coercions that endanger the persuasion process. The degree of coercion is to be proportionate to the necessity, and, within the magnitude required, is to be economical of all values.

(12) To provide for outcome procedures in which the primacy of the whole personality over component roles is given effect (territorial over plural authority, e.g.)

(13) To maintain outcome procedures that give effect to rational interpretation and assessment of information

The foregoing outline provides a frame of reference for considering many of the questions that arise in searching for the formulations to be incorporated into a constitutional charter. The formulations by no means exhaust the modes of considering the problems involved that are helpful to policy scientists and concerned participants. The following analysis, for example, narrows the focus to a fundamental dimension of the problem of planning power allocations. *How does one clarify and give effect to common interests and to the resolutions of uncertainties and conflicts among them?*

For convenient exposition we consider first some principles that relate to the allocation of authority. They are followed by principles of control.

1. *Arrange for common interests to prevail over special interests.*

The problem of obtaining the primacy of common over special interests is the fundamental and perennially troublesome problem of all allocations of authority and control. The principle draws attention to the many structural solutions that have been adopted in historical situations as means of discovering and adhering to the common interest. The procedural solutions are closely interconnected: *first, involve all interests actively all the time or on particularly important occasions; second, involve third-party representatives of the common interest in other situations.*

If all the members of a body politic were equally motivated and able to participate actively in all decision processes, and if they did in fact so participate, the common interest would presumably achieve maximum expression. According to tradition, this state of affairs was actually realized in the New England town meetings of a certain period, and also in many folk societies. In many circumstances, however, direct universal participation is prevented. For example, the poor and uneducated may not take the time, or may be too handicapped to express themselves effectively. Or the population may expand until a town meeting becomes unmanageable, and mass media of communication, such as television, are not yet adapted to the requirements of politics.

, One adjustment to limited active participation is *representation*, either by vote or appointment. If the representatives are motivated to act on everything, and the decision process makes this possible, representative government can achieve the common interest as effectively as direct democracy is able to do, when it is operating under the most advantageous conditions. Experience suggests that in complex societies representatives are continually being multiplied, as more problems press for resolution. Representatives may be multiplied by direct election or by delegating nonelected officials to assist elected representatives. Elected bodies, such as legislatures and councils, try to cope with the pressure of demand from the environment by using committees to give detailed consideration to proposals that would otherwise be unexamined.

It is no secret that the division of labor provides opportunity for common interests to be clarified and realized more effectively, coupled with opportunity for special interests to confuse, distort, and defeat the realization of common interests. So far as the furtherance of common interests is concerned, the *multiplication of man hours of attention devoted to decision problems renders it possible, if community predispositions and capabilities are properly sampled, to arrive at a view of the common interest in whatever matter is given consideration. If motivations and capabilities are sufficient, the decisions can be arrived at in the light of the knowledge and estimates available.* A simple model for common verus special interest decision processes follows:

Demands→	Man-hours of→	Samples of→	Mobilization→	Decisions with
for	decision ac-	community	of available	common or
decision	tivity (direct	predisposi-	knowledge	special interest
	participants;	tions and		dominant
	representa-	capabilities		(acceptable,
	tives-commit-			realistic)
	tees, officials)			

The *demands for decision* originate among participants in the political process who are either inside or outside official institutions. The *man-hours of decision* refer to the total structure of the arena in which political decisions are made. *Community predispositions* are the perspectives of identity, value demand, and expectation, while *capabilities* refer to the base values of all kinds available to decisionmaking officials or agencies. *Mobilization of available knowledge* refers to the strategies employed by decisionmakers in attempting to arrive at the outcome that disposes of particular problems. The *outcomes* are classifiable in terms of common or special interest, degree of acceptance, and reality. The latter term, reality, refers to estimates by scientific analysts of the validity of an interest through time, that is, whether the effects sought will be or have been realized.

The analysis makes more explicit the point that where direct representation is not feasible the problem of power allocation in an authoritative charter is to encourage the primacy of common over special interests by two strategies: (1) obtaining "third-party" decisionmakers—those who are not immediately involved in conflicting claims—by recruiting them from samples of the whole community's distribution of predispositions and capabilities; (2) fostering the demands and capabilities required to mobilize pertinent knowledge.

Among the possible formulations designed to further the first objective are (1) provision for review of specific recommendations by bodies of diverse composition (e.g., subcommittees by larger committees, committees of the whole); (2) disqualification of final decisionmakers having special interests relevant to the issue (e.g., judges, members of regulatory agencies); (3) public records of deliberation, votes, explanation of votes (e.g., publication of proceedings, open sessions, judicial opinions); (4) explicit negative sanctions for putting special above common interests (e.g., disqualification and dismissal, double indemnity for gains); (5) providing assistance in maintaining independence (e.g., payment of officials); (6) protection for or freedom of reporting criticism, of assembly, petition, political party, and pressure organization.

Among the arrangements relating to the mobilization of knowledge are (1) support of official libraries, laboratories, field expeditions, staff planning, and policy development agencies; (2) notice and hearing, official inquiries, subpoena authority; (3) consultative and advisory services.

2. Give precedence to high-priority over low-priority common interests.
Policy makers do not have sufficient guidance in reference to common interests unless they are provided with indications of how they are to be ordered under various contingencies. Some common interests are particularly important because of general agreement among members of the body politic on ranking. In traditional societies many locations are held in great reverence, and if support is to be obtained for technological change, it must be made explicit that cemeteries are not to be plowed under, and that shrines are to be protected. A critical issue is the balance between investment and democratic consent, which poses problems of timing the steps toward freedom and prosperity.

3. *Protect both inclusive and exclusive interests. Give preference to inclusive interest when protection of the purportedly exclusive interest involves significant value deprivations of the larger community.*

Common interests are inclusive to the degree that a policy affects the value position of all community members directly. An exclusive interest may involve a few members very gravely, but have insignificant repercussions for others. The common interest is served by a public order that protects freedom of choice and leaves as many decisions as possible to parallel actions outside the realm of *direct* collective action. *Parallel* actions may, however, have consequences that remove them from exclusive to inclusive interests, as when parallel acts of environmental pollution are significantly involved. A formulation that establishes an initial presumption in favor of exclusive action has the advantage of making it necessary for the larger community to be mobilized for action when evidence accumulates about aggregate involvement. The presumption can then be overcome.

Many devices have been employed to protect an exclusive presumption of interest without preventing inclusive action from being taken as the factual situation changes. Constitutions may be open to amendment, but the procedure may be more difficult than is required for ordinary legislation. Majorities may be required on two occasions a year apart, for example, or exceptional majorities (e.g., two thirds) may be prescribed. An initiative and referendum procedure may initiate a general election.

4. *Give preference to the resolution of conflicting assertions of exclusive interest by the participants whose value position is most substantially involved.*

Since we give priority to individual and subgroup choice in the body politic, basic policy formulations should encourage the settlement of conflicting claims that refer to exclusive interests by the parties most substantially involved. The larger community is not necessarily concerned with the particular value consequences at stake in a given dispute. It is, however, deeply concerned that conflicts should be resolved without damage to public order, and particularly without coercion. Provision is therefore made for community decisionmakers to be available to the call of parties to a conflict that they have not been able to cope with between themselves. This is the *supervisory* function of government, and is exemplified in litigation over private contracts or wrongs. When the deprivation is perceived as an attack on the norms of the community in addition to whatever damage may have been done to particular individuals, a collective sanctioning or *corrective* function is executed by government. *Regulatory* functions involve norms that private activities are to abide by, and which, if alleged to be violated, may be dealt with by actions initiated by public or private persons.

The community decisionmakers who deal with regulatory problems are notoriously liable to betray common for special interests, since the commissions involved are targets of continuing inducement and threat by the particular activities they are supposed to keep within limits. The assets at the command of large corporate organizations are available bases for all forms of influencing activities. Regulatory activities often pass through cycles:

Active public demand →
   Establishment of regulatory structure →
      Diminution of public attention and initiative →
         Deviation from norms   →
           Official inaction   →
              Growing protest   →
                Active public demand culminating   →
                  in new structure, etc.

Swings in the cycle can be abbreviated if interests can be consolidated in support of effective regulation. Therefore a serious problem of the formulaters of authority and control is to find ways of strengthening the appraisal function. One device is to provide for a full-scale legislative review of regulation by automatically terminating the regulatory prescriptions every ten or fifteen years. Another expedient is to provide for annual assemblies by organizations drawn from immediate and more remote interests (consumers, suppliers, workers, researchers, etc.).

5. In addition to authority, allocate base values of sufficient magnitude to enable authority to be controlling.

Theoretical analysis based on experience emphasizes the point that provision must be made for values other than formal authority to be obtained if control is to be effective. A clause delegating authority to an agency must therefore be sustained by clauses that allocate the assets, in addition to authority, that are needed to enable the recipient of authority to do what is required. Money, for instance, is not formal authority; a claim to money is. And a claim to money is an instrument whose effectiveness depends on the future mobilization of money assets. Unless words generate words and deeds that amass resources, they will fail to set in train the sequence of relevant events. Power allocations must provide so far as possible for base values of a range and scope commensurate with the task to be performed. Representative provisions are for taxation and borrowing, and possibly for the operation of revenue-producing enterprises.

The assignment of authority must include access to enough arenas to strengthen the likelihood that political control will be proportionate to authority. This may involve a guaranteed post in the cabinet and membership in interdepartmental committees. More generally, *the primary decision function to be performed must be accompanied by a degree of participation in all functions.* This may imply authorization to operate a separate intelligence service, to control a chain of communication media, and so on.

Looking beyond the official organs, it is evident that a given agency needs a *constituency* in the social process that will provide for the continuous mobilization of the demand necessary to operate effectively. If the common interest is to be protected and fulfilled, the mobilization process must include a coalition that adequately samples the community.

The problem of the designer of power structures is to discover relatively *coherent* and *independent bundles of activity* that can provide (1) a continuing focus of public attention and (2) a discernible constellation of common identity, values, and expectations. Such an independent operation may combine official and semiofficial decision arrangements.

Instead of burying the operation in a department it may be set up as a visible *authority* with a separate executive responsible to a council selected by a combined territorial and pluralistic constituency (e.g., the International Labor Organization). Medicare, education, environmental protection, nuclear power, transportation and communication, and savings and loan services are among the possibilities to be considered.

Although the preceding pages have focused on public authority and control, policy scientists face somewhat parallel problems when they are asked to play an advisory role in established governments or in revising the fundamental charters of associations that are semiofficial or private, such as political parties, pressure (interest) associations, foundations for scientific research, business corporations, private health facilities, schools, family arrangements, prestige societies (e.g., to confer honors), churches, and so on.

Each client must operate within the framework of public authority and control unless it is committed to revolutionary or criminal purposes. It is not, of course, essential for the client to accept the existing state of public order, since as a participant in the social and decision process he may decide to change it by utilizing legally acceptable means of promoting change. The policy scientist is especially qualified to assist in clarifying and executing objectives of the kind.

Clients must institute a decision process internal to their own operations. Some clients are formally "private" yet so interwoven with the lives of the community that the separation does not exempt them from many of the considerations that affect public structures.

From the standpoint of public policy every permissibly independent operation pursues the *common* interest of the community by engaging in its *exclusive* interest activities. Taking the private organization as a context, it is essential to find criteria and procedures for distinguishing the common interests of the organization from special interests, and for giving effect to the former. It is important to distinguish between common interests that are *inclusive* (and therefore appropriate for organization-wide implementation) and interests that are exclusive (and appropriately left to decentralized or deconcentrated decision). The resolution of uncertain boundaries between exclusive interests within the organization present problems parallel to official community structures. The fundamental power allocations call for the supplementation of formal authority with authorized access to other base values commensurate with formal authority.

Among the client services that the policy scientist can perform is assistance in resolving controversies among participants in private organizations over the interpretation of such charters as the articles of incorporation, collective bargaining contracts, and so on.

CHAPTER 7

Professional Identity

Introduction

Indispensable to the growth of the policy sciences is a network of institutions adapted to the objectives of the profession. In this chapter we discuss the problems that arise in evolving an intelligence function that enables policy scientists to supplement their individual sources of knowledge with a common data pool. We also assess the public and private images of policy scientists and the nature of the roles to be played, not as advisors, but as principals in the public decision process.

A Knowledge Network

Much of the know-how of any discipline is disseminated orally and by means of personal exposure to exemplars who provide a range of positive and negative models. Since training institutions and professional firms differ greatly from one another in competence, prestige, and other attributes, opportunities for learning are not equally distributed. Specialized media of communication inside the profession help to mitigate such inequalities, and to conserve and expedite the whole body of theory, method, and practice.

Publications include communications of varying length, purpose, and content, utilizing different media, and addressed to different audiences. More systematically, in the communication process *who* initiates and controls, for what conscious and unconscious *goals* and objectives, in what *forums,* with what *assets,* using what *strategies,* to reach what *audiences,* with what *effects?*

To begin with the *who* question, the distinctive initiators of what is available in technical journals will presumably be members of the profession (and its cognate groups), together with appropriate professional associations, teaching, research, and consultative agencies. In a relatively pluralized society the control of professional applications will continue to lie in the hands of qualified private individuals or organizations, who also add knowledgeable and dedicated persons chosen from the wider environment.

The goal of the publication network will be to serve policy science objectives. These can be formulated according to the effects sought on audience members who are inside or outside training situations. In spatial terms objectives can be classified as directed at transnational or local targets. Temporal references may be topical, aimed at the immediate past, present, and future; or they may be concerned with middle- or long-range periods in the past or future. Objectives are also classifiable according to the value-institution sector or problem-solving task concerned.

In principle, the forums appropriate to policy science publications are divisible into four widening circles: members of the profession, members of other professions who provide knowledge for policy, professional clients, members of the community.

What can be accomplished by any communicator depends in part on the assets available to him, particularly the degree of enlightenment and skill, and the technical network at his disposal. As the prestige of policy science rises, talented and ambitious young people can be expected to turn to it in increasing numbers.

The impact of publications, even on a highly motivated professional audience, is affected by the strategies employed. The strategies include a media mix of printed, audio-visual, and personal channels, and a range of special modalities, such as treatises, periodicals, or information storage and retrieval systems.

The choice of audience for the network depends on the potential forums enumerated above. The strictly professional audience is divisible into students, teachers, researchers, practitioners, and related roles. Men of knowledge who have little interest in decision process, though intensely involved with particular problems of public policy, present a distinctive challenge. Similarly, distinctive handling is required for actual or potential clients, and the members of national, transnational, and subnational communities who follow the lead of policy scientists.

When communicators are true to their basic viewpoint, they insist on appraising their effective impact. They search for the function most appropriate to any mode of publication. Although computer technology provides a means of storing, retrieving, and processing data, it has reformulated rather than eliminated many problems of communication.

Core Periodicals

Consider, for example, the role of *periodicals* (and periodical equivalents) in the emerging network. The connotations of a periodical are legacies from the age of print, and include (1) publication at regular intervals, (2) cumulation of issues to approximate the length of a book, and (3) presentation in each issue of articles that contribute to the principal objective of the enterprise. In nonprint media, article equivalents include expository programs within the period at the disposal of a given channel (such as news and comment over radio-television facilities, or a regular lecture).

Connotations slack off toward larger or smaller elements in the total flow of communication. Units less than an article (or article equivalent) are *notes, abstracts, summaries,* or *items,* for instance. Larger units include *brochures, books,* or *program series.*

A preliminary question is whether periodicals and articles will survive in coming years as forms of publication. They can be expected to continue as long as the following points are accepted by the professional community: (1) the usefulness of occasional summaries that exhibit the "contours" of the field (thus standing between primary data statements and the most inclusive systemative formulations) and (2) the convenience of having new contributions made accessible at frequent intervals. Articles may be in prose, or prose may figure more modestly than statistical tables, charts, pictures, maps, or exhibits. A computer network is capable of presenting results in many forms. It is probably safe to predict that prose essays will diminish (to a minimum level) as other modalities are better developed and gain wide acceptance.

A *core periodical* performs a central rather than a peripheral function in the principal forums with which the policy sciences are concerned. A central role implies (1) a unified context and (2) a distinctive audience. The two chief responsibilities of the policy sciences are for (1) knowledge of decision and (2) knowledge in policy areas. The principal forums, as indicated above, are the profession, other knowledge professions, clients, and fellow citizens. At all times the fundamental approach is contextual, problem oriented, and methodologically diversified.

A core periodical designed to meet the needs of the profession by providing a selective view of the whole field provides a place for articles intended to clarify the distinctive frame of reference of the policy sciences, formulate the principles most fundamental to its evolution, disseminate contributions having wide appeal, and report and evaluate all that is most pertinent to professional development. The recently launched *Policy Sciences* magazine has an opportunity to play a central role.

Periodicals will undoubtedly be initiated or adapted to meet the needs of policy scientists who are concerned with the policy process in the main territorial and pluralistic contexts of the globe. Territorial contexts will continue to reflect the prevailing divisions in the world community (cultures, races, regions, subregions, etc.). Another specialization among core periodicals will presumably emphasize each of the five intellectual tasks. In turn, these may be differentiated by territorial and pluralistic categories: symbolically, Policy Sciences of Philosophy, History, Science, Projection, and World Public Order.

Hopefully the core journals that serve the policy sciences will be edited *integratively,* rather than in *omnibus* fashion. The omnibus style of publication is an inadequate though once useful step toward a wider frame of reference.

The omnibus style can be illustrated from practically every journal of self-identified specialists devoted to any one of the sciences of culture. For instance, the principal organ of the American Political Science Association is the *American Political Science Review.* It publishes articles from all the recognized subfields of the discipline. Often a specialist in a subfield, like political parties, is looking for an improved technique to apply to a problem such as how political parties formulate their policies toward other parties. A study of the intelligence function in national government may inspire new and rewarding research on the intelligence process in party systems. If the omnibus journal were not published, the specialists on a given subfield would presumably stay out of touch with developments in neighboring fields much longer. Predictions based on the theory of least effort suggest that the omnibus journal makes it easier for members of the discipline to follow developments in all fields than if it were necessary to read several journals.

Although the omnibus technique of juxtaposing articles from several subfields in a single magazine is partly successful, it is not necessarily the most efficient means of accomplishing the purpose. The policy science frame of reference suggests a different approach, and one that places a heavy responsibility on editors. Their role is conceived as organizing attention in such a manner that promising methodological innovations in all fields, ranging across political science to all the cultural, biological, and physical sciences and arts, are included. Besides searching for procedural innovations, editors need to look for contributions that raise promising and neglected questions. Journals can report on these matters without waiting for a fellow specialist to complete and publish a book.

The policy science approach implies that every core publication of a given profession can be edited in ways that link the specialty with the context. It is, for example, commonplace to observe that for a time historians are likely to overlook emerging questions and techniques that can be fruitfully applied to the past. The central journals for those who specialize in history, if they are edited in a policy science perspective, will explore developmental constructs of the future and indicate some research implications.

The editorial challenge to those who edit the core journals in major problem areas is similar. The policy science of wealth, education, and so on calls for a roving editorial eye that brings the hidden agenda of every group of specialists into the open.

The third set of core journals—those designed for the nonspecialist—pose a difficult editorial task. The predispositions of any professional field are known to fellow specialists. Beyond such a group lies the entire social environment with its complex array of territorial and pluralistic groups. Of particular significance for public order are those who are likely to play an active and influential part in the decision process at every level. The policy science profession does not fulfill its larger goal unless it assists in consolidating a network of communication facilities that aid in disseminating pertinent information and in mobilizing demands to act effectively in its utilization. This implies that the editors of media for external audiences are relatively more concerned with motivational problems than their opposite numbers in charge of internal media.

The motivational challenge has many implications. Consider groups whose members are predisposed to "keep up with the policy sciences," and who provide an audience for journals and articles that differ from most professional media in the simplicity with which the basic message is presented. Many models are to be found in science reporting, such as *Nature* in Great Britain or the *Scientific American* in the United States. In the field of economic policy the London *Economist* had a remarkable role for many years.

As one moves away from the *stably motivated* audience, any attention given to the findings or methods of a professional discipline is *episodic*. The general audience of a mass medium of communication is sensitized by recently shared experiences, such as news events with wide coverage (moon landings, heart transplants, and so on). These audiences also share many of the recognizable identities (e.g., age, sex), value demands (e.g., concern about health), and longer-range expectations (e.g., the threat of racial conflict). The Paris *Match* or the *Reader's Digest,* for instance, summarizes special knowledge when it is judged to appeal to the topical or the permanently "human." Besides the general audiences there are the particular audiences whose episodic willingness to hear about specialized knowledge depends on a timely link with their opportunistic preoccupation with particular interests. The thousands of pressure associations and other private organizations in a large industrialized society belong to the vast network of fluctuating audiences.

A question for the policy sciences is whether the controllers of general and particular media are willing to approach their responsibilities in a policy science frame of reference, and whether, if so, they are willing to identify themselves with the goal values of human dignity. Are they able and willing to involve their readers and viewers in a policy science orientation?

Encouragement of Continuous General Participation

A feature of the policy sciences approach that we recommend is general participation. In no sphere of life is the participatory emphasis more fundamental than in relation to the public media. The problem can be considered in reference to expanding circles of interaction.

The most solvable problem is how to bring knowledge specialists into efficient collaboration with experts who are skilled in communication. This presents little difficulty when the assignment is to prepare articles for a stably motivated audience. Educated journalists are available to cooperate with willing scientists in the preparation of a mutually acceptable text to be published under the name of the scientist or the writer, or both. The form may be an interview or a straightforward exposition.

Traditionally the specialized scientist has been somewhat reluctant to acquiesce in the "mutilation" of his results in the short and vivid presentations often appropriate to general media. Presumably the emerging generation of policy scientists will be sufficiently alert to the importance of cooperation to reduce collaborative difficulties to a minimum.

More problematic is the transformation of passive or episodic audiences into active and continuing participants in the policy processes, including the conduct of research analysis, and systematic appraisal.

Many individuals respond actively to the media as a source of intelligence about the world. Some write letters to the editor, repeat fragments of a story in casual social contact, or clip and file selectively. Not many take the step of utilizing the information to prepare a comprehensive chart and map room for themselves or the family, or for some other group to which they belong; or of inviting the interested collaboration of others in interpreting trends and projections, and in considering the alternatives open to them. It is more common for clippings or recordings to be kept and filed by an employee. The next step—the preparation of a chart, map, and conference room—is rarely taken. Hence the prevailing image of the relevant whole is not subjected to active assessment and revision.

Librarians of communities, schools, businesses, and other public and private organizations have not accustomed themselves as yet to play an affirmative role in assisting their constituencies to take a more active stance toward knowledge and policy.

The controllers of mass media are in a position to cultivate motivation for continuing involvement. Many school and neighborhood clubs are interested in both photography and the community. It is feasible to organize competitions on a local, regional, national, or even transnational scale to encourage comprehensive, selective, and vivid documentation of past trends. These activities and awards can be supplemented by similar initiatives intended to encourage imaginative future projections and plans.

These practices can be encouraged by cautious, middle-of-the-road interests. Many youth and reformist groups would also perform a public service if they would use the film to document such violations of law as the buying and selling of drugs, or the giving and receiving of pay-offs for "protection." Existing equipment is sufficiently tiny to allow the photographer to provide explicit and detailed evidence of the actualities of life at every level. Such material can be disseminated through nonsubservient channels of public communication. The documents and documentaries add circumstantiality to vague rumors about graft and inefficiency in public or private organizations. A contextual, problem-oriented conception provides guidance for general participation in the intelligence and appraisal functions of the body politic.

The communicators can plan and encourage the preparation of background material for use in putting current happenings in a meaningful context.

Not one, but several, program planning and commissioning agencies can be used—or set up—to speed the preparation of television library material on a world scale. The programs would be available for use before much time has passed, but the chief aim is to devise programs worthy of inclusion in the quasi-permanent television library of the cross-national system. For the most part the programs can be historical and analytic. The agencies can be selected to specialize on different parts of the social process:

1. The history and analysis of man as a biological form, and of the main movements of culture and civilization.

2. The history and analysis of power (government and law), with reference to the emergence of institutions that protect individuals from official or unofficial arbitrariness.

3. The history and analysis of science, with reference to the diffusion of knowledge.

4. The history and analysis of media of general communication, with reference to the "right to know."

5. Economic institutions, with reference to productive levels and gradation of benefit.

6. Well-being institutions, with reference to the safety, health, and comfort of the masses as well as classes.

7. Skill institutions, including the arts, vocations, and professions, emphasizing opportunity to acquire and exercise skill.

8. Institutions of kinship, family, and friendship (affection) with reference to range of choice.

9. Institutions of social class and caste (respect), with reference to mobility.

10. Institutions of religion and ethics (rectitude norms and practices).

The participatory approach to public media exemplifies one of the principal objectives of policy scientists. The aim is to subordinate the particular interests of a profession to the discovery and encouragement of public interest. This implies direct community participation as well as client service.

Participation versus Bureaucratism

Seen in this context, the use of media to encourage continuous and informed participation on the part of general audiences is a fundamental strategy for coping with many fundamental difficulties in our society. Among the difficulties *bureaucratism* has a high place, and this is closely associated with the appearance of *oligarchy*. Bureaucratism is a term that designates the many ways in which large-scale organizations fall short of their opportunities, and produces negative results in the community. Oligarchy is the concentration of power in the hands of a few, a process that encourages and is encouraged by bureaucratism.

Modern instruments of communication—the computer and the mass media—can be utilized to mobilize decentralizing and pluralistic demands in large-scale organizations. The essential principle is that a *picture of the self-in-context can be made available to participants at every level of formal authority from top to bottom of every hierarchical arrangement.* If the chart and map room technique mentioned above can become generalized throughout society from earliest to latest years, the chances will be greatly improved that enough motivation will be sustained to allow for widespread participation in policy processes. Hence the antidote to bureaucratism and oligarchy lies with the motivational and informative potential of communication.

As usual when questions of social change are raised, the problem is whether latent tendencies can become manifest in perspective and in deed. And this is a challenge that policy scientists feel called upon to assist in answering.

And this raises the identity issue.

A Distinctive Identity

The distinctive outlook and synthesizing techniques of modern policy scientists are interwoven with the evolution of a distinctive identity image. The conception of the policy sciences is at once a by-product of an emerging image and a contributor to its further clarification.

The contemporary policy scientist perceives himself as an integrator of knowledge and action, hence as a specialist in eliciting and giving effect to all the rationality of which individuals and groups are capable at any given time. He is a mediator between those who specialize in specific areas of knowledge and those who make the commitments in public and private life (the public and civic order). He is continually challenged to improve his theory of the policy process itself, and therefore to perform a crucial role, especially at the intelligence and appraisal phases of policy.

In achieving the new identity it has been necessary to overcome the image of a second-class man of knowledge and a second-class man of action, and to perceive that the integrative role of the policy scientist is indispensable to the security and advancement of a world civilization of science-based technology. The scientist or scholar who becomes the mediator between the social environment and his colleagues is a target of ambivalent sentiment on the part of colleagues and the larger environment, and privately he often shares the ambivalence. Fellow specialists may think of him as a careerist, as a man who tries to substitute power for serious achievement. Presently they regard him as an ex-scientist or ex-scholar. The larger environment is not certain how to categorize a man who stands for knowledge and is nevertheless a man of affairs. As a man of affairs, the dean or the president or the association secretary or the consultant seems half-hearted. He is not necessarily a standard-brand politician who runs for office or manages a party machine. He is sufficiently intellectual to arouse some inferiority feelings among men of affairs, and he is enough of a man of affairs to introduce a note of constraint in the intellectual community. He is perceived as "half man, half brain."

Both the intellectual community and the community at large are beginning to acknowledge the indispensable place of the integrator, mediator, and go-between. However, the appropriate image is still semidefined. Perspectives are in flux.

And indeed this somewhat confused, contradictory image is not out of harmony with the present state of transition. The basic uncertainty is, Whose side is he on? Presumably policy scientists as a whole can be analogized to one of the traditional practitioners of the mediating role, the lawyer. The lawyer is "for hire"; hence he is permitted to serve the presumptively guilty as well as the presumptively innocent. But there are limits on his freedom. He is, after all, an officer of the court, which gives him a semiofficial capacity. There are limits on the strategies that the counselor is permitted to use on behalf of a client, and it is perhaps vaguely perceived that public policy goals are served by giving everyone who is involved in a public controversy an expert who can say whatever there is to say on his behalf. Obviously, this may bring to the focus of attention of the community decision-maker data that would otherwise be neglected. Hence it may serve rationality.

It is pertinent to examine once more the larger context in which knowledge and men of knowledge are involved.

At least one fundamental statement about our time arouses little disagreement: The science-based technology of Western European civilization is moving toward universality. Almost everything else is open to debate. For instance, is the man of knowledge taking over the seats of the powerful? Will he? Should he? Such questions give new vitality to talk of professional ethics, or the social responsibility of science, or the control of education and research.

That political power is affected by knowledge and that political power affects knowledge are no revelations. The interesting problem is the timing of two-way effects. Until recently it could be held that knowledge affected power more slowly than power affected knowledge. A substantial change in the map of knowledge would first alter many less comprehensive maps. Then technology changed, altering the composition and experience of groups. The resulting changes in the direction and intensity of demand affected public policy. Political decisions, in contrast, have often had immediate consequences for knowledge. If proposed appropriations are voted yes or no, everyone—researcher, teacher, or student—adapts as well as he can.

Today's timing is different because the structural position of science is different. The impact of new knowledge on public policy is almost instantaneous, thanks to the many institutions that specialize in science or government, or mediate between the two. A huge communication network interconnects laboratories, observatories, field stations, and libraries in universities, industries, and governments. Revised matter-of-fact expectations, such as comprise the map of knowledge, promptly change expectations about the future of all concerned. As a result policies are modified: Scientists suddenly see new lines of research, technologists recognize promising lines of development, investors see new investment opportunities, officia's perceive new ways of affecting national security (or insecurity). Given the position of science in American or Soviet society, the chain runs from innovations in the map of knowledge to projections of the future, to evaluations of alternative policy objectives and strategies, to demands for decision, to the making of decisions, to further changes in perspectives, behavioral operations, and aggregate structure.

Science, Militancy, and Oligarchy

Despite the remarkable, even explosive, expansion of knowledge, and its global diffusion, it must be conceded that, up to the present, the aggregate impact of the scientific revolution has failed to revolutionize the basic structure of world politics. The relations of the United States, Soviet Russia, and mainland China, to say nothing of the middle-sized and smaller powers, are constrained as usual by the expectation of violence. The expectation of violence contributes to, and is in turn sustained by, the division of the globe into apprehensive or threatening powers in an arms race of unexcelled magnitude and danger. This divided and militant structure of the world political arena preceded the era of science, and has succeeded thus far in subordinating the institutions of knowledge to its perpetuation.

We take note of another fact about the social consequences of science. It is often pointed out that knowledge is more commonly used for the relative benefit of the few than for the benefit of all. This is most obvious in the contrast between the suburban ghettos of the prosperous and the poverty-stricken ghettos of urban and rural slums.

How can we account for the historic subordination of knowledge to the institutions of war and oligarchy? Certainly there is no lack of hortatory rhetoric on the part of eminent contributors to knowledge celebrating the latent universality of the fruits of knowledge for all mankind, or the fraternal unity of all who contribute to a verifiable map of nature, man, and society.

Up to the present a root difficulty appears to be that however universal the manifest content of scientific propositions, or the procedures by which they may be verified, they are parochially introduced. Their diffusion or restriction is heavily dependent on the characteristics of the parochial environments in which they appear. The response of each environment depends on the expectations of advantage or disadvantage that would follow from expediting or interfering with the global spread or technological application of new knowledge. It is a matter of everyday experience that most individuals and organizations are not interested in the advancement of knowledge as an end in itself either for themselves individually or collectively. They are concerned not with enlightenment as a scope value but as a base for obtaining wealth, power, respect, health, and other valued outcomes. In a world divided by the institution of war the support for science depends in no small measure on the expectation that scientific knowledge will contribute to the power needed to throw off the domination of imperial states and to achieve a level of modernization that will prevent the reimposition of direct or indirect rule from outside. Among the superpowers and the older industrial nation states, science is cultivated to provide the muscle that is presumably required to maintain freedom from enforced subordination to outside control.

The institution of war is expressed and sustained by drawing scientists into a coalition with political leaders, military officers, administrative officials, factory managers, and other significant participants in the power process. In socialist-communist hierarchies the coalition mates are the top leaders and bureaucrats of the monopoly party (or political order), the political police, the army, the official departments and agencies. In bodies politic having more co-archic traditions and procedures, much more prominence is given to the leaders of private industry, competitive political parties, pressure groups, and mass media of communication. The military-industrial complex is no respecter of popular distinctions between forms of industrial society.

The Inner Structure of Knowledge Institutions

Why science works for power can be better understood if we examine the inner structure of knowledge institutions themselves. We recognize that scientists differ from one another in the intensity of their commitment to fundamental theory. At one limit are those who specialize on the principal contours of the map of nature, man, and society; at the other are routineers who fill in detail. The former are oriented toward enlightenment. Typically their skills include techniques of theory formation and procedures of primary observation directed to novel possibilities. Those who fill in detail are more characteristically equipped with skills adapted to purposes other than fundamental enlightenment. The implication is that, as the pursuit of verfiable knowledge grows in importance in society and research institutions expand, the percentage of those who are mainly concerned with fundamental enlightenment diminishes (toward an unknown limit) in comparison with those who are satisfied to exercise their skill in the service of other purposes. As the knowledge institutions expand, they reach a level at which they recruit personnel from all save the most humble strata of society. Hence *the personnel of science increasingly comes from those who share the conventional culture, which means that knowledge is seen as instrumental to value outcomes other than the pursuit of enlightenment.*

The consequence for the subserviency of science to political power, or to other "practical" values, is evident. Those who, in effect, "have skill, will move" make themselves understood and available to the demands of decisionmakers at every level. These are the mid-elite and rank and file of science and scholarship. From them are recruited the thousands who cement the interdependence of science and the established structure of society. In the aggregate they contribute more directly to the service of war and oligarchy than to world security and the welfare of the whole community.

It is true that from their broadly based supply of manpower the scientific establishment does succeed in developing a relatively small and highly respected elite whose members are oriented toward knowledge as an end in itself, or as an end that ought to be employed for the benefit of the whole nation of man rather than its parochial subdivisions. Many members of this elite are specialized to operations whose working techniques are less than usually dependent on the empirical data collected by the individual investigator, or on immediate applications. Included are many mathematicians, logicians, linguists, and related theorists who are less firmly embedded than their colleagues in the constraints of a localized environment.

Highly Capitalized Science

The dependence of science on the social environment is emphasized by the transformation from the early age of handicraft science to the present era of highly capitalized science. The flow of assets for research and education depends on sustaining a structure of expectation in the environment that "knowledge pays." Hence the internal structure of knowledge institutions changes in ways that enable them to draw upon the environment. In the subculture of science those most directly responsible for these expectations are those who mediate between the institutions of knowledge and other institutions. They include heads of laboratories, department chairmen, deans, presidents, popular professors, many trustees, public relations and development officers, alumni secretaries, and the officers and staffs of professional associations.

The participation by scientists in the decision processes of society goes much further than in representing the case for the support of science. The fact is that the decision processes of modern and modernizing powers are deeply permeated by men of knowledge. The proposition is true even when you eliminate the lawyers and theologians, and count only physicians, scientists (physical, biological, behavioral), and engineers, or those who have received college or professional training. It is true of many political leaders, government officials, and military officers in industrial and industrializing countries.

All this has happened, yet the institutions of war and oligarchy continue. Evidently, we can have scientists in government without having government for science or man. Along the path that leads from an early training in science toward political leadership or government service the individual learns the conditions of survival in the arenas of power. He learns to negotiate behind the scenes and to propagandize in public places. The outcome is a present politician and an ex-scientist, a man who has learned to survive by coming to terms with the militant structure of world power and the typically oligarchical structure of internal politics.

Visibility and Vulnerability

The bearing of this evolution on the future of science in society is far from trivial, for science has grown strong enough to acquire visibility, and therefore to become eligible as a potential scapegoat for whatever disenchantment there may be with the earlier promises of a science-based technology. Even today there is much articulate disenchantment that goes beyond the traditional resistance of feudal elites to industry and science-based technology. If the earlier dream was a rising tide of production, the later reality also includes the social costs of polluted air, water, and soil. If the earlier hope was the abolition of disease, the current reality includes the discovery of pharmacological side effects that threaten life and health. If the earlier dream was safety and security for all, the current reality is the augmented peril of nuclear or biological destruction. If the earlier dream was that latent capabilities would be identified and matured into socially useful skills, the present reality includes augmented public and private forces of organized militancy, criminality, and delinquency. If the earlier vision was that destructive limitation on the growth of love and dedication would be dissolved by knowledge-guided socialization, the current reality is a very considerable demand to dominate, or to withdraw, to nonparticipate, to self-segregate, to celebrate alienation from collective life. If the earlier promise was that knowledge would make men free, the contemporary reality seems to be that more men are manipulated without their consent for more purposes by more techniques by fewer men than at any time in history.

Are we, in fact, in another period in which the faiths, beliefs, and loyalties of a once progressive evolution have so weakened the bonds of public and civic order that massive seizures of destructive rage at the humiliations imposed on human dignity will once more disrupt the nonviolent processes of change, and reinstate the turbulence of a time of trouble, a rebarbarization of civilized centers, and another collapse of a discredited system of militancy and oligarchy? The verdict may be that whom the historical process would destroy it first must make strong enough to achieve a visibility sufficient to arouse false hopes, while remaining weak enough to acquiesce and connive in the frustration of their potential—thus for science and scientists.

Current Proposals

It must not be supposed that all men of knowledge, and notably scientists, are happily reconciled to the contemporary situation. Many of them resent the degree to which their knowledge builds political power for others, or accumulates wealth for others, while leaving them to enjoy an advisory status quo and a fluctuating income from charitable gifts or bureaucratic salaries. In our society more specialists are taking steps to work for themselves rather than for others. They often use the corporate device of limited liability to set up profit or nonprofit companies in the hope of benefiting from entrepreneurial gains. Consultants and consulting firms often take their compensation in the form of stock, enabling them to share the appreciating assets of a successful enterprise.

Another and often closely connected source of dissatisfaction is the resentment among scientists of the degree to which they seem to be working for the benefit of an oligarchy instead of contributing directly to mankind.

Many of them are searching for forms of scientist and user cooperatives that pool knowledge and technical know-how in laboratories that generate products and services for the general welfare.

These sentiments cut across the parochial lines of communist-socialist or liberal-capitalist economies and politics. Do we, in fact, stand at the beginning of a movement that could transform the role of science? What if every university or every professional specialty had exclusive claim to the discoveries and inventions of its members so that an increasing share of the applications of knowledge would flow to the man of knowledge? Would he work directly to spread the benefits from science to raise the aggregate level of regional and national welfare, to call a halt to the diseconomies of environmental loss, and especially to undermotivation for the use of human resources? In a word, would the scientist work more directly for man?

We are not without historical precedents of at least limited relevance. Some monasteries—Buddhist, Muslim, Christian—have sustained their rituals, their charities, and their scholars by marketing alcohol or other commodities. A modern university occasionally supplements its income from the proceeds of a patent or copyright pool. It is not inconceivable that associations of scholars might publish all the textbooks and reference works in their field, and design and manufacture educational (and hopefully interesting) games and school equipment. The school of architecture and planning might design cities.

More than this, associations of scientific planners might take the lead in developing a transnational chain of cooperatively organized cities intended to aid the formation of a new world community within the framework of the old. Perhaps cities can be built on old or new islands or space platforms for people who "opt out," as far as possible, from the arms race. Perhaps great enterprises for the development of resources can create nonsegregated communities in the present waste regions of the earth (the deserts, the polar lands). Once constituted, such centers could reach well beyond their nominal boundaries and provide educational, scientific, recreational, and medical facilities for many more people than they would accommodate as permanent residents.

Are Scientists Like Everybody Else?

It is not too difficult for us to identify some of the factors that explain why proposals of this kind have made relatively modest headway. For instance, there is fear of their implications for the internal policy process of professional associations and universities. Any multiplication of entrepreneurial functions would multiply administrative staffs and presumably alter the balance of impact on decision. It is feared that those who engage in the activities that bring in the most money would insist on increasing their weight in the decision process. Many are apprehensive that conflicts would both proliferate and intensify over the identity of acceptable outside contractors; the salaries and conditions of work of researchers, teachers, administrators, and students; the allocation of resources for expansion in the physical, biological, and cultural sciences. One can envisage interuniversity competition to attract the big money-makers (as well as grant-swingers), or to set up new splinter associations in order to improve the "take" by the professional skill groups in relatively short supply. Also, it is not difficult to imagine competing horizontal unions appealing separately to younger, middle, or older faculty members, or to recent or older students, and confronting one another as collective bargainers. As the knowledge institutions extend transnationally, it is not absurd to predict the accentuation of cleavages among rich and poor and according to traditional identities of tribe, language, race, or nation. In a word, the pessimistic expectation has been that a scientist or any other man of knowledge will act like everybody else, especially if he (or his spouse) thinks that he has a chance to get a bigger piece of pie somewhat nearer than the ever receding sky.

Let us grant that this conventional wisdom has more than a grain of truth as a description of the past. Will it necessarily be true tomorrow? Is it to be asserted as beyond dispute that scientists and institutions of knowledge will continue to fail to identify and to serve common interests within the field of science and humanity?

Cognitive Maps and Procedures

Perhaps, as some colleagues suggest, the challenge actually calls for a basic reconsideration of the character of the cognitive map for which it is appropriate for science to take responsibility. The proposition is that the fragmented cultivation of skill for opportunistic purposes is not enough. It does not automatically trigger an invisible hand that redraws and improves the contours of the general map of knowledge. A truly comprehensive cognitive map would include the significant future as well as the salient past. The inclusive map becomes known, not only by the piecemeal splitting of the pebbles on the beach, but by identifying the changing contours of sea and shore.

The proposition is that at any slice of time these aggregate contours are the principal realities of nature, life, and culture. They are also the entities that in the past we have been least successful in identifying, explaining, or managing. It may be that, as we adopt methods appropriate to discovering the congregation of cycles that define the reality of the moment, we learn how to modify their future timing by feeding their symbolic representations back into the intelligence flow of the moving present.

If attention is to be directed to the relevant cognitive context, appropriate institutions must be invented or adapted to the purpose. Luckily, we are not without guidance in this matter. For example, we are becoming accustomed to the planetarium technique of providing a selective audio-visual experience of the past and future of the earth and its environment. We are capable of adapting the technique to the presentation of equally inclusive and selective maps of the past and prospective succession of biological forms. It is entirely possible to apply the planetarium technique to depictions of the past, prospective, and preferred sequences of value priorities and institutions in the social process of the earth, the hemisphere, the region, and the neighborhood.

It is not difficult to see how these contextual techniques can be adapted to the task of providing a regular means of giving consideration to the social consequences and the policy implications of knowledge. Such a function can be performed by a continuing seminar concerned with a provisional and changing map of the past, present, and future of science and man. Whatever the specialists represented, the practice of sharing, evaluating, and contributing to an inclusive map keeps alive the latent embers of concern for the knowledge enterprise as a whole.

Here is a means of examining the historical trends, conditioning factors, and future projections of the impact of knowledge on the use or abuse of human and environmental resources, on the institutions of war and peace, of production and distribution, of safety and health, of education and family life, of social caste and class, of ethical or religious responsibility, and of the future of science and scholarship themselves.

We recognize the possibility of feeding into a perfected network of interconnected seminars and planetaria the results obtained by the most sophisticated simulations of past and future (area by area, component by component).

Such changing cognitive maps can be used to initiate and guide the formation of research policy by identifying the zones of neglect or duplication.

These presentations can release creative policy proposals for the future structure and functioning of universities, the professional associations, and communities at every level.

Common versus Special Interests

Furthermore, these continuing seminars can be incorporated explicitly into the whole complex decision process of professional associations, universities, and other knowledge institutions. These primary centers of cognitive orientation provide at least a partial answer to the challenge issued to men of knowledge by the conventional wisdom that the scientist and the scholar are as incapable as other men of discovering and pursuing enlightened common interests. If men of knowledge cannot run themselves, how can they expect to continue to be taken seriously by the rest of the community as advisors or leaders? The argument is that if we cannot find criteria and procedures for discovering how, within the community of science and scholarship, common interests can overcome special interests, we cannot be trusted to clarify common interests in the wider community.

As indicated before, the possibility is not to be overlooked that the task of eliciting and evaluating the policy objectives and alternatives open to professional associations, universities, and other knowledge institutions will bring about a progressive improvement in fundamental cognitive maps and in the scientific process itself.

Furthermore, we can think in terms that include continuously expanding arenas of cognitive and policy operations. They may well begin inside knowledge institutions, and then proceed to the decision processes of mixed knowledge and other institutions at national, subnational, and transnational levels. Certainly if political power is to be shaped and shared outside the limits of oligarchy, and if coercive authority is eventually to be supplanted by a voluntary civic order, it is fairly clear that the members of the body politic must have the means of keeping their cognitive maps adapted to the discovery of valid common interests, and of mobilizing dispositions to do what is necessary to overcome the dominance of special interests. In the circumstances of today's world, men of knowledge, especially men of science, can participate, as many are already doing, with the victims of urban blight and total neglect in a mutually illuminating search for the timing of the policy objectives and strategies that overcome these discriminations. Specialized men of knowledge, in cooperation with neighbors in the opulent suburbs, can search for the cues that release latent dispositions to overcome indifference to, or satisfaction in, the plight of others. In conjunction with the peoples affected, scientists can strive to identify the timing of the acts most likely to close the frustration gap that separates the multitude in underdeveloped nations from their newly awakened hopes. Most challenging of all, perhaps, is the possibility of continuing efforts to discover the timing of options that tame and redirect the militantly competitive elites of the opulent and knowledgeable powers, and to integrate a system of world public order that serves, not merely the minimum requirement of security, but the optimum potentials of man and his resources.

Career Patterns

The discovery of how to navigate through the future calls for the perfecting of institutions of knowledge that are as yet poorly adapted to the knowledge of time or the timing of knowledge. The individual man of science may continue to devote himself mainly to the exercise of the competence for which he is trained; or he may complicate the pattern of his career by life plans that combine specialized activity with varying degrees of role playing in the decision processes of public and private institutions. In any case he can make these continuing policy judgments for himself, and in conjunction with others, with higher hopes of realism and relevance if he engages in recurring reappraisals of cognitive maps that display the social consequences of knowledge for the aggregate shaping and sharing of valued outcomes, and the readjustment of social institutions.

The emerging careers open to those men of knowledge who propose to mediate between knowledge and action include the specializations that conform to the conception of policy scientist. His role is to improve our knowledge of collective processes of decision while taking active measures to improve the use of knowledge in decision. Therefore he utilizes one or many roles that include professional advice to public and private clients, and direct participation in all the decisionmaking and decision-executing roles available in society. In adapting to these possibilities it is evident that the identity problems of the policy scientist are as complex as those of anyone in the world community. Presumably the contextual, problem-oriented, and methodologically integrated approach contains the seeds of continuously creative resolution.

CHAPTER 8

Professional Training

Introduction

Not many full-time policy scientists can be identified at present, partly because the conception of the policy sciences has been more latent than actual. This is, in fact, a period in which, as was pointed out in the first chapter, the basic approach is emerging in the minds of many people. It is hackneyed though probably true that this is, indeed, an epoch of explosive development in which many converging streams are bringing coherence into the field, and inaugurating a series of overlapping and promising programs and institutions specialized to the training and education of policy scientists.

It is characteristic of new or revolutionary conceptions and professions that no one or very few individuals embody a "perfect" exemplar of the ideal image. In our expanding world it seems wise to lay aside the temptation to emulate Jehovah, who is believed to have created man in his own image, and to adopt the modest aim of shaping a social role in the image of what we would like to become, or to see more perfectly realized. In the early days of the policy sciences the training problem is to establish environments that contribute to the formation of persons who copy no single model, and who integrate the better features of each partial approximation.

The pitfalls are numerous and it is to be predicted that many initiatives will fall short of the goal. For example, it is highly probable that the kind of integrative synthesis recommended in the present book will tend to disappear in many of the programs and training schools that adopt the term *policy sciences* or a closely related symbol of identity. There are many inducements to allow the inclusive emphasis to disappear. Where rewards seem to follow localization, any attention to the inclusive context may offer few visible advantages.

Nonetheless, some factors tend to keep alive concern for a contextual, problem-oriented, and methodologically diversified approach. Societies with a complex map of knowledge provide at least some rewards for those whose chief value is enlightenment. Little maps are always invitations to look at bigger as well as smaller maps, and some individuals are predisposed toward bigger maps. We honor the man who modifies established assumptions. In the conventional miranda of our world we are trained to revere the Galileos, the Darwins, the Einsteins, and the Plancks. True, the system heaps up counterincentives and deferred incentives. The drastic innovator may suffer neglect during life and achieve secular immortality when he is dead.

Given the rate of expansion of the whole stock of knowledge, it cannot be denied that the individual pursuit of enlightenment would seem to be a losing game. In the traditional figure of speech, knowledge is compared to the growing sphere that comes in contact with ever-enlarging areas of ignorance. However, the implied conception of knowledge is not altogether appropriate. Knowledge can be described in at least two dimensions. One is *accretional,* as exemplified in the statement that several billion new descriptive details are added every few seconds to our store of data about the earth's environment. The other conception is *contextual* and emphasizes the clarity with which the principal contours of the celestial system can be concisely and validly presented. The search for contour is as deeply embedded in our make-up as the search for detail.

In principle, there is no reason why practically all human beings cannot share an approximately equivalent conception of the world. Notions of *whole* and *part* are inseparable, and it is greatly to the credit of some communication scientists that they are tackling the equivalency problem at all levels of aptitude and experience. Admittedly the specific details available to the totally blind or the color blind are very different from the details available to the fully sighted person. But the total configuration of an ego's experience occurs in a process of interaction that allows him to make inferences about other egos on the basis of many kinds of data. It is a happy commonplace to recognize that Aunt Mary may not need to count every grain of sand in order to conclude that the beach is sandy. However, the planners of the Normandy invasion of Europe needed to know much more than Aunt Mary will ever need to know about the precise nature of variations in sand. They sent over landing parties to bring back sample after sample of the beach. The implication is that the degree of detail appropriate to a person at any time depends on the problem. A shared public map can be magnified or microfied.

Every enlargement of the map of knowledge generates a specialized interest in particular domains. We predict, however, that specialized groups will

continue to include at least a few individuals, who with even small incre-
ments of encouragement, will keep alive an active concern for the whole.
One aim of the emerging policy sciences is to provide incentives for this
group.

Context and Specialty

The relationship of policy scientists to the expansion of knowledge is twofold: one, the recruitment of integrators from every emerging specialty; two,
the provision of a shareable orientation among all people at any level of age
and exposure to culture. The first is the challenge of professional training.
The second is the challenge of public education.

Diagram 1 is a crude representation of what is involved:

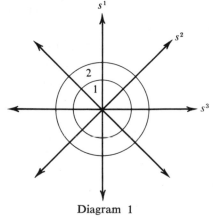

Diagram 1

The intersecting lines (s^1. . .) stand for the specializations of knowledge. Any number of such lines may be needed. The larger circle (2) includes the policy scientists who are recruited from those who cultivate any
particular specialty. The circle enclosed by line 2 refers to what is known as
well as to those who know it. The circle includes an inclusive representation
of knowledge in which every specialty has a place. The size and contours of
the map are constrained by the time available to specialists who prepare a
comprehensive map of where their specialty fits. The inner circle—defined
by line 1—also refers to a group and a map. The group is composed of
those who comprehend and transmit an intelligible map of knowledge to all.
The size and contours of the map are drastically constrained by the inflexi-
bility of the time periods available at the focus of general attention.

The interconnections among the various bodies of knowledge can be shown by emphasizing the three principal frames of reference that preoccupy men of knowledge, and the dual emphasis put on arts and sciences. The three divisions are the physical, the biological, and the cultural sciences and arts.

The physical sciences are physics, chemistry, astronomy, and the earth sciences; and the physical arts cover all the technologies by which physical events are deliberately manipulated for purposes other than fundamental enlightenment. In this category are the engineering technologies that exploit the characteristics of elementary particles and states in their various combinations.

The biological sciences are the study of the common characteristics of all living forms and of the species-bound traits of individuals. The biological arts embrace all the technologies by which living forms are manipulated for purposes other than primary enlightenment.

The cultural sciences are the study of behavioral patterns of living forms; the cultural arts are the techniques by which these patterns are manipulated for purposes other than primary enlightenment.

Diagram 2 provides an indication of the way in which a university structure might give relatively direct expression to the contextual and specialized map of knowledge. By tradition a university is chiefly oriented toward conserving and expanding the stock of knowledge. Hence enlightenment is the principal value in terms of which its activities are appraised. Universities are also concerned with the utilization of knowledge in realizing all the values of man. It is the recovery of this comprehensive conception that gives new vitality to the search for institutions suitable to the highly differentiated state of knowledge and the organized characteristics of civilization.

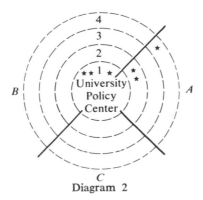

C
Diagram 2

The University Policy Center (1) formulates plans, and supervises execution and appraisal. The *sectors* (*A, B,* and *C*) are the three broad fields of knowledge: cultural sciences and arts, biological sciences and arts, physical sciences and arts. Despite the differences shown in the size of these three sectors, no inferences need be drawn concerning the importance or the magnitude of resource allocation to these sectors of the map of knowledge.

The Division of Unified Programs (2) arranges context courses and programs in different areas, provides personal orientation to students and others, and guides efforts to appraise the consequences and policy implications of knowledge.

The Departments of Science (3) are in each appropriate sector (e.g., physics, zoology, economics).

The Schools of Arts (including technologies) (4) are in each appropriate sector (e.g., electrical engineering, agronomy, business administration).

Centers, Departments, and Schools

The diagram presents the field of knowledge as a whole and indicates that the functions of a university can be classified in the four circles corresponding to the policy process of the institution, the preparation of unified opportunities for the exposure of all to the map of knowledge, the organization of departments responsible for the systematic and analytic growth of each sector and subsector, and the schools specialized to professional training in the management of knowledge for social goals and objectives.

The University Policy Center is not to be confused with the Policy Sciences School or Policy Sciences Center. The University Policy Center is part of the structure of a particular university and faces the distinctive problems of the institution. A School of Policy Sciences is focused on the training of professionals concerned with the general field outlined in the present book. The single asterisk on the diagram indicates that such a school fits into the sector specialized to the cultural arts.

The conception of a Policy Sciences Center is not identical with a School of Policy Sciences, although in some circumstances a center may be closely connected with a school. A center does not take full responsibility for professional training, which is the task of the school, although training may be supplemented by a center at postprofessional or other levels. The distinctive role of a Policy Science Center is indicated by the position of the two asterisks in the diagram of a university where the center is located in zone 2, where it figures as one of the structures included in the Division of Unified Programs.

The conception of a Policy Sciences Center provides a frame within which policy processes can be studied and knowledge can be related to public policy problems. A center is designed to be small enough for the participants to interact with one another in a creative intellectual manner. In recent decades the idea of a center has been evolving as a means of counteracting the fractionalizing of knowledge in universities, where the proliferation of departments and schools has gone unchecked. The most important innovation was the Institute for Advanced Study at Princeton. It has been adapted to other purposes at the Center for Advanced Study of the Behavioral Sciences at Palo Alto. Another offshoot has been the growing practice at some universities of providing for off-campus scholars and persons of experience to join with some members of the local faculty for a year or more free of routine duties.

We also note the potentiality of a planning and appraisal structure located in the first ring of the University Policy Center and designated by three asterisks. Any university has its own problems, and the inner circle might well include a *subcenter specialized to the problems of planning and appraising the specific organization.*

A further differentiation is important in large organizations where it is wise to separate the intelligence (planning) function from appraisal. In connection with the analysis of government we emphasized the advantages of separating appraisal from planning. Planning agencies, like every structure, can be expected to develop a self-serving bias that reduces the credibility of the appraisals that are made of the success or failure of its own plans. In smaller organizations it may be a sufficient guarantee of realism to arrange for an outside advisor to appraise selected features of the plans initiated by the "in-house" agency.

Qualifications

When we think in terms of a School of Policy Sciences, it is necessary to face the question of student (as well as faculty and trustee) qualifications. Consider first the school that is located in circle 4 of sector A (cultural arts of technologies). In the ordinary academic sense it would be treated as coordinate with law, public administration, business management, schools of education, welfare administration, public health administration, science administration, and so on. The school would draw on individuals who have had training in the departments of the cultural sciences (circle 3) or who transfer from other schools in the division. It would also reach across to the biological and physical disciplines and attract students who aspire to the mediating role between a specialty and the development of policies that take the social consequences of knowledge fully into account.

Some centers can be independent of the structure of a particular university and can be designed to meet the needs of policy sciences in general or of territorial and pluralistic contexts. The former might engage in a variety of professional services for clients ranging across many social institutions and localities. Individuals might move back and forth between such independent structures and the training and research environments of universities, or the policy sciences organs of official or unofficial organizations. In all cases provision might be made for a program of professional training that would be certified by an academic degree or appointment as a fellow in a professional society. Similarly the responsibility for accrediting the adequacy of a particular school or program would require an agency satisfactory to the emerging profession.

The selection of students for policy science training is a matter of balancing motivation and capability with the facilities available at any given time. Motivation is especially important, since it enables an individual to endure the risks of a partly accepted role. Relatively novel careers appeal to somewhat different students than do the standard professions. The policy sciences conception will provide many talented and public-service-oriented young people with an attractive challenge.

If we are to judge from current expressions of interest, the career will seem promising to those who have become disenchanted with standard professions that are closely related to policy. A common complaint is the overloading of students with detail that seems but remotely related to policy formation and execution. Law school curricula have been packed and repacked with course requirements that derive from the rapid proliferation of specialized activities in modern society. The tendency of every decisionmaking structure is to generate its own bar, and to favor the introduction of courses in the legal curriculum, and to add another hurdle to bar examinations. Law teachers find that a course that meets the approval of a particular bar contributes to the teacher's professional prestige in some quarters and provides a market for students in search of job opportunities. The usual routine is the preparation of journal articles, case books, and special journals to assist in consolidating the field.

There is no valid objection to be raised against the development of professional specialization. There are, however, valid objections against poorly integrated professional training. If the specialty were coupled with a policy science approach to relevant contexts, something new would be added to legal education. Consider, for instance, the study of the law of communications which, though a rather new course topic, is responsive to the appearance of the Federal Communications Commission in the United States. If the course were a guide to the comparative study of legal institutions and public policies toward communication in all countries (or a well-chosen sample) and in transnational regions and jurisdictions, it would provide an excellent grounding in relevance. However, when courses in communication law that duplicate conventional methods of analysis in other courses are added to the curriculum they add little but memory work and intellectual fragmentation to legal training.

A parallel multiplication of courses that add factual baggage in place of enlightenment is characteristic of many, if not most, graduate and professional schools in government, public administration, economics, business administration, sociology, welfare administration, and many other areas of advanced study.

Many of the students who are in individual or joint revolt against excessive requirements are searching for a curricular experience that corresponds to the policy sciences approach, and are likely to find most welcome a school that lives up to the approach.

Not all rebels are rebelling in ways that parallel a policy science frame of relevance. Far from demanding less detail and more relevance, the critics may be opposed to any tendencies toward "theory" that occur in required courses. This response is conspicuous among students whose family origins include skilled workers, small businessmen, and the more modest professionals. For such young people abstractions often seem to waste time; the demand is for bread-and-butter courses that seem to prepare them to pass qualifying examinations for the civil service, and teaching, or for jobs in private practice.

Many of the most prominent rebels in recent years are contemptuous of the attitudes expressed by both the "upward mobile" lower-class student, or the student who is interested in "relevant" disciplines. These rebels are opposed to any disciplined intellectual approach whatever. Instead of dropping out of professional training they attempt to stay around universities and to contribute to the disorganization of any sustained intellectual program. The effort may be justified in the name of "intuition" or the "mind in communion with itself." In the absence of knowledge the communion connects one vacuity with another, and cannot be said to have any promise for the policy sciences.

New programs usually appeal, not only to students of high competence and creativity, but to misfits who lack what it takes to pursue any profession seriously. Schools of Policy Science will find it necessary to protect themselves from the glitteringly garrulous with no habits of work, from the self-righteous pluggers who combine vast industry and modest talent with mild fantasies of persecution, and from similarly unpromising applicants.

Many otherwise admirable students will be poorly motivated or poorly prepared in mathematics, and will therefore find it difficult to meet the level of competence appropriate to the comprehension of operations research and other complex techniques. Many applicants with an easy command of mathematics, statistics, and logic will show no aptitude for comprehending the strategies of communication or diplomacy, or, in general, for achieving structural change by modifying current conceptions of the common interest.

Those in charge of schools or programs in the policy sciences will find themselves exploring many intermediate positions between relatively stringent or permissive criteria. In the next few years it should be possible to discern criteria of selection that integrate the contextual requirements of policy science with high levels of aptitude for particular operations within the context. Those who strive to keep alive and to make effectively operational the inclusive viewpoint will remind themselves of the high intellectual standards appropriate to each of the philosophic, historical, scientific, projective, and inventive tasks; they will recognize the tension between advisory and full participatory roles, as well as between teaching, research, and more immediate decision-shaping operations.

An analytic look at historical situations will confirm the variety of paths that have led to the performance of functions that are more or less strictly equivalent to policy science roles. They will no doubt search for those who combine motivation with some exceptional capability or some unusual mix of exposure to configurations of culture, class, interest, personality, and levels of crisis.

The Uses of a Prospectus

An institutional practice that seems useful to schools or programs in policy science is the comprehensive prospectus. The essential idea is to encourage self-guidance by providing the student with a detailed preview of the field as conceived by the responsible faculty. Such a prospectus would outline (1) career opportunities, (2) theoretical conceptions of the field, and (3) sequences of preparation. The guide would include a selective and up-to-date annotated bibliography of the policy sciences, in this way enabling the student to expose himself to the subject in an order that appeals to his level of interest, knowledge, and experience. The prospectus can be simplified and adapted to the needs of preprofessionals, and of postgraduate practitioners who keep with it.

Integration: Study and Field Experience

It is generally recognized that training will be most effective when it provides for a balance between opportunities to read, reflect, and discuss, and opportunities to participate in a variety of field situations. The two polar dangers are well known: the concern with library research that produces the passivity of mere erudition, and the preoccupation with reality that duplicates the conventional roles in society's current cast of characters. Professional training is in perpetual tension between the scholar, thinker, theorist, book man, or contemplator, on the one side, and the clinician, manager, man of action, or manipulator, on the other. A policy science school will continually appraise the effectiveness of its past and recent emphasis on the contemplative and the manipulative.

Integration: Problem Orientation

The polarities to be organized in a training program are much more complicated than the rather rudimentary, though ubiquitous, contrast between study and field experience. The five intellectual tasks are in unstable balance, and any tendency to lose sight of one or another will weaken the whole approach. The problem of professional training is to see that each task is well represented, and to search for faculty who keep distinctiveness without losing contact with associates. Recall the goal clarifier who moves into philosophic or theological preoccupation, the describer of trend who is permanently intrigued by the past, the analyst of conditioning factors who focuses entirely on explanatory questions, the forecaster or predictor who is absorbed in the world of tomorrow, or the policy inventor and appraiser who is committed to the fifth intellectual task in the analytic list. It may be wise to include in the basic charter of a school the requirement that these several specialties shall be represented. This will serve as a permanent re-

minder of goal, and call attention to any changes of direction that seem justified in the future.

Crosscutting the five tasks are differences that may be far apart though
held in partial equilibrium, such as the concern for an inclusive or a narrow
context in "time, space, or figure" (the latter term covering the patterns of
the social or universal process within time and space). A goal clarifier may
concentrate on the objectives of all living forms or of man alone, or of any
subset of men down to the smallest partnership, neighborhood, or family. A
historian may search for developmental constructs that embrace all history,
or deal with the immediate and the parochial. A scientist may converge on
data from past or present, or plan for future observation; and he may range
from explanatory models of macro to micro processes. A projector of future
events may extend or restrict his scope; so, too, may an inventor or evalua-
tor of policy alternatives.

A further dynamic tension can be distinguished, this time among those
who utilize one or another of the many methods available to policy scientists.

Integration: Personal and Situational Contexts

Another set of potential opposites can be effectively interrelated, namely,
the distinction between the inner and the outer look. In extreme instances
the former is introspective and concerned with insight into the individual's
private world; the latter is extroverted and concerned with *things* and *persons*. The contrast is often between a deeply meditative approach and an approach that "acts out" long before it "thinks out" or "feels out."

The challenge of the policy sciences is to encourage an integration that
approximates the complex model of which man is capable in his role of
contemplator and manipulator, of problem solver in the inner or outer
world.

The Continuing Decision Seminar
as a Technique of Instruction

The contextual character of the policy science approach calls for the development of approximate instruments for problem solving as well as for instructional purposes. The basic requirements of a seminar adapted to the
policy scientist's task have been described before. A decision seminar for instructional purposes deals explicitly with the theory of decision, including

the operation of the seminar itself. The *continuity* criterion implies that the decision seminars of a professional school bear no necessary relationship to the coming and going of the student or even the faculty population. The critical requirement is a *nucleus* of persons who are determined to work together over a number of years. There may be some change in the nucleus, but not enough to break up the undertaking. Other participants may come and go, sometimes as full members, often as expert witnesses or collaborators on limited tasks. A decision seminar may cultivate *spin-off groups* to concentrate on related problems, and to communicate from time to time. The seminar may also encourage coordinate groups to concern themselves with the same basic problem or with specific technical operations. For instance, a *technical seminar* may devote itself to the choice of operational indices for all governmental activities, and to the designing of storage and retrieval networks. Or a seminar may concentrate on a single intellectual task in reference to a selected historical or contemporary body politic. The following titles indicate what is meant: "The Philosophy of Democracy," "The History of the Police," "The Effect of Chemicals on Behavior," "The Comparison of Projective Techniques," "The Limits of Zero-Sum Models."

Decision seminars are not limited in principle to governmental institutions. In fact, it is not possible to put governmental agencies in proper perspective unless they are compared with private institutions that operate in the same social context. This inference follows from the interactive character of social process, and from the impossibility that any specific structure can monopolize the shaping and sharing of any one value (power, wealth, enlightenment, etc.).

Policy training programs may be directed toward the needs of institutions other than government. Hence they will emphasize counterpart seminars chosen with reference to the sector of the social process on which they specialize.

The traditional university is specialized to enlightenment, which is the advancement of knowledge. Policy science programs deserve to be in universities to the extent that they live up to the requirement that they contribute to the advancement of knowledge *of* and *in* the decision (policy) process. Specialized policy science programs emphasize the first criterion, which is knowledge *of* the process. Every scientific and professional school needs to cultivate awareness of the social consequences and policy implications of knowledge in general, but with special reference to the knowledge closest to their competence. Continuing decision seminars provide a means by which specialists can be reminded throughout their careers of the social consequences and policy implications of knowledge. Such an instructional device can enable them to maintain a degree of awareness of the larger social context on which they depend, and with which they perpetually interact.

Seminar Requirements and Procedures

We are now in a position to consider in detail the requirements and procedures that distinguish the continuing decision seminar technique from other instructional devices. We have emphasized the preliminary requirement of a *small nucleus* of self-constituted members. The accent is on a committee or panel rather than a legislative-size assembly or congregation. The nuclear standard is proposed as a means of focusing full responsibility on the problem in hand, since common experience tells us how often the degree of involvement in a collective undertaking varies inversely with the size of the membership.

Closely related to this criterion is the *determination to continue*. The contrast is with "one-shot performances" or with committees having a rapidly shifting membership, where the discussion must be kept on an introductory and general level, and where experience is not cumulative. In this connection it is to be stressed that the recruitment of a self-motivated group does not always occur quickly.

A university environment is relatively rich in specialized talent, but it is notorious that the traditional academic person is an individualist trained to search for new truth, hence to challenge accepted opinions, and to search for novelties that justify his claim to original discovery. Cultivating the mind is an elusive career, partly because the external behavior of the creative person often provides no dependable clue to what goes on inside his brain. There is some reluctance to adhere to a schedule that obligates one to think about the same thing at the same time. Hence in university circles it is often a complicated operation to build groups that are unified in problem and purpose.

Several approaches have been partially successful in achieving unity under various circumstances. When the graduate faculty of the New School for Social Research was organized in the thirties in New York City, it was composed of professors who had escaped from Germany and Italy. They were sufficiently unified by their experience to celebrate the importance of human freedom and to understand the fragility of the factors that sustain it. They were united by concern for, and commitment to, the knowledge enterprise as a whole; and they found it congenial to meet as a faculty seminar to consider the wide range of questions in which all were interested. The faculty seminar was not a true decision seminar, since it lacked a sufficiently defined frame of reference. But it provided a seminal situation in which congenial minds could discover one another and eventually collaborate on particular matters.

A more structured arrangement developed at Columbia University, where participation in a faculty seminar was fully accredited as part of the course obligation of an interested faculty member. Many articles and books have taken shape in these seminars. Although interdisciplinary in composition, the exercises on Morningside Heights have rarely been true decision seminars, since they often lack a future-reference orientation.

Interest in the future is no guarantee of continuous and coherent involvement in decision seminars, although a *future* seminar is often an important step in enabling teams of interested colleagues to spin off and work together. A recent experience at Yale is illustrative. During one year a group of faculty members from different departments outlined future developments in their areas of competence (China, the Soviet Union, youth, etc.). After a year the feeling was that the group should delimit the field, and the result was a number of group activities, some of which began to approximate fully developed decision seminars.

After the motivation requirement is met, the path is open to arrange for a sufficiently high *frequency* of meeting to maintain progress on the common task. In practice this standard can be met in many different ways. There may be periods of joint activity at daily, weekly, or forthnightly periods; or circumstances may indicate the wisdom of a longer rhythm. The latter is especially important when the members are widely dispersed and can only come together at some cost. Specialists on global regions, for instance, are likely to be divided between those who are at their usual headquarters (e.g., university, institute, official post) and those in the field. As institutions of advanced education become more accustomed to off-campus activity, the problems of joint operation assume less formidable proportions. And this would presumably be characteristic of advanced policy training programs. Field expeditions are already an ordinary feature of many law and graduate schools, and are increasingly acceptable during part of the traditional academic year. For a long time American anthropologists have given major emphasis to the importance of knowing how to gather data in the field, and a comparable practice is spreading through neighboring social sciences.

The *internship* practice, for example, is well adapted to the purpose of supplementing campus experience. Political scientists in the United States, for instance, have explored several arrangements of the kind through their professional societies. Internships have been available for a year or more at every level of government—federal, state, and local. They have been adjusted to the needs of legislators and legislative committees, of executives and administrators, and of political party and lobbying organizations. It has long been customary for the justices of the Supreme Court and of other courts to hire law clerks who serve as apprentices for a year or so. This technique has also been extended to the courts of developing nations, notably in Africa.

Although these arrangements perform an important educational function for the individuals involved, and generate personal ties that foster promising careers, internship programs are open to some objection. The chief difficulty is that the apprentice can become so absorbed in his task that he loses the analytic perspective, which is what prevents him from becoming another political hack or a petty clerk. This difficulty can be overcome by the continuing seminar technique, because auxiliary seminars can be developed to accommodate the needs of interns. A continuing workshop or seminar on the key committees of Congress, for example, can be organized at a university with a nucleus of professors, alumni, and off-campus figures who keep the undertaking alive. They can use *auxiliary seminars* to accommodate task forces whose term of activity is relatively brief. By utilizing the auxiliary seminar or task force device an intern can be confronted with the challenge to cope analytically with his experience, and to discover how it can be used to contribute to a basic problem (such as following the trends of institutional change, and anticipating their presumptive lines of growth).

Frequency, then, is a programmatic detail of great though variable importance for decision seminar technique. A more complex requirement is the *commitment of seminar members to a disciplined and contextual program.* This expression is intended to suggest that much more is implied than occurs in what are traditionally called seminars.

The seminar of academic tradition does, however, carry some connotations that are worth keeping, and which justify perpetuating the name. A seminar is a group in which *everybody works on something new.* The usual image has been for a professor to guide the research of students who are mature enough to contribute to the advancement of knowledge. In practice, seminars shade off from the ideal image in many directions (as when pedestrian summaries of the present state of knowledge are tolerated). A seminar may move toward a research team of equals in which the apprenticeship or teaching feature vanishes. Or the research project is so tightly defined and executed that younger participants become research assistants of the principal figure, who may have no interest in encouraging independent approaches to the central or allied problems.

The decision seminar technique adds something to the fundamental demand and expectation that everyone will be at work on something new. As we have said, a seminar is supposed to *use procedures that enable its members to contribute to our knowledge of decision or to evaluate the significance of knowledge for selected decisions.* Hence whatever the scope of the undertaking it is conducted with this *theoretical responsibility* in view; and to be in view implies that it is *explicitly emphasized throughout.*

Assume, for example, that the exercise is planned to be a *counterpart* seminar that parallels a structure of government. One recurring question would be what light the study has thus far thrown on the general theory of decision, or, more narrowly, on the factors that affect the functioning of a certain category of the structures in the power process. In the course of its activities the seminar would explore interconnections between the structure and the other structures in the political process (also interconnections with structures in the social context outside the sector specialized to the shaping and sharing of power). The five problem-oriented tasks would be dealt with (goal, trend, condition, projection, alternatives). In a highly approximate agenda for seminar meetings these theoretical tasks would be taken up in recurring sequence.

In any case, presentations by individuals to the group would make use of audio-visual aids, and deposit charts, graphs, or related material for subsequent sessions. The employment of *audio-visual devices* is no idle exploitation of decorative ideas. The maps and charts are helpful means of storing and recalling information. The sight of the relatively permanent visual material recalls the original presentation, including the discussion. Hence the group develops in more cumulative fashion than is otherwise possible.

Every policy seminar evolves its own *audio-visual environment.* Sometimes a very primitive allocation of exhibit space on the walls of a room is a unifying step. For instance, one such seminar devotes one wall to analytic charts outlining the social process model, the decision model, and the five problem-solving tasks. It also contains a map of the earth's environment in space, which is drawn on a scale that expresses distances as multiples of familiar dimensions in the earth's immediate environment. The wall also exhibits a map indicating the broad lines of the earth's evolution as a habitat for living forms. The space might well include a projected future for the earth and cosmos. (At present the input of information from radio astronomy and space probes is rapidly modifying our accepted notions. The principal models are in lively debate.)

The remaining wall space in the seminar is apportioned to two sets of presentations, one serving as a reminder of the social process categories as they refer to the world community, the other to decision functions. The convention is established that eye level is the present, and that the arrow of time flies from the floor to the ceiling. Hence past trends and conditions are located below; future projections lie above. Material that deals with the future includes *passive projections* of things as they are likely to be, and *preferred projections* of goals and strategies.

In some seminars the stock of accumulated visuals grows slowly, since one procedural principle is to *give priority to material that has been prepared and introduced by members of the group itself.* This is part of the "do it yourself" strategy designed to counteract the tendency to "think by delegation," and to hear reports from "experts." Seminar members benefit from taking responsibility for a presentation and for preparing themselves to disclose the sources on which they rely and the interpretations that they prefer to accept. A reporting member may actually be an accepted expert in the field of his principal presentation, although this is not always an advantage, since his very expertness has probably led to built-in biases connected with the particular school of economics, politics, or sociology, for instance, where he was trained.

Many means are available to nullify or weaken the effects of bias. The basic procedure, of course, is the *critical examination* of the original presentation by all the members. Another is to hold a session where an outside specialist is invited to act as an *expert witness,* not as a permanent member of the cast.

No restrictions are placed on the sources or the method of reporting adopted by a particular member. Some reports may bring together the results of an original research conducted on a transnational scale with ample public or private funding. Supporting documentation may be circulated in advance or after the initial discussion. The visual material may be presented as slides projected on a screen, or made available as a "card pack" to each individual. And what is chosen as the principal continuing exhibit may be a tiny part of the total report submitted for the *permanent files* of the seminar, which may include *tie-in arrangements* with data storage and retrieval systems, and consoles where seminar participants can immediately and directly manipulate data. In some instances a continuing seminar can evolve a huge *social planetarium,* where the semipermanent exhibits are prepared and evaluated by the group. Films can be prepared and kept at hand to assist the enterprise as its members "live their way" into the past and future.

Whatever the procedures adopted for exhibits, the crucial point is the experience of the members of the seminar in ordering their focus of attention in a contextual and problem-oriented sequence. Hence *a feature of each presentation is the giving of explicit attention to the interconnections of the items under discussion.*

For instance, if the seminar is located in a divinity school and is devoted to the policies of an order devoted to religious training, some reports will undoubtedly deal with educational trends, conditions, and projection. Others will help to evaluate their significance for policy alternatives intended to contribute to the realization of the overriding goals. Trends in instruction can be clarified by the act of relating them to corresponding trends in other religious settings, and in secular society. Any explanation that is offered of factors that affect the direction and magnitude of trends can be evaluated in the light of comparative researches inside and outside the institutional system. The hypothesis that "strictness" in requiring work to be completed is a factor in any falling off of interest in religious interaction may be abandoned if it can be shown that strictness is welcomed when it is associated with new techniques of presenting old material, such as gaming. Alternative future policies may include the question of how religious training programs can conceivably make a welcome contribution to the several sectors of society — political, economic, and so forth. Following such procedures can bring new questions to mind and pave the way for a whole new set of proposals. For instance, it may be suggested that a religious order should undertake preschool education in child care centers, where working parents can leave their youngsters. This proposal requires careful evaluation in terms of its technical requirements, prospects of support, and repercussions on the place of religion in the community.

It may be that a policy seminar becomes so impressed with a particular set of possibilities that it *alters its original plan* drastically in the hope of obtaining an important new result. A seminar on the urban political process, for example, may find itself absorbed by rediscovering the importance of "protean man," as Robert J. Lifton calls the modern character with no strong inner system of value-tactical orientation. This may lead to an examination of the "alienation" phenomenon, and to the suggestion that prototypical projects can throw a bright light on the way in which young people can experience a strong sense of community. Or if the initial seminar was on the topic, "Energy Sources in the World of Tomorrow," it might find out about the potentials of solar energy and decide to become a study and promotional group dedicated to the marshaling of support for world action on behalf of a satellite capable of supplying the energy needs of man indefinitely, and doing so free of the pollution connected with fossil fuel.

Because of the enormous importance of *cultivating creativity,* it is probable that many decision seminars will explore ways and means of stimulating novel and realistic innovation. The essential strategy is provided for in the procedures outlined above, since the principal provocation for creativity is exposure to incomplete or inconsistent contours in a general map of reality. An artist is sufficiently skilled to resolve the clashing lines of landscape and factory, or the incompatible colors of posters, flowers, and dumps. A policy-oriented person can perceive contradictions between advertising that presents high consumption standards as an implied reward of personal charm, and the prevalence of moralistic admonitions to cultivate attributes other than charm. The significant question is, How does one proceed to modify the balance, if one decides to try?

Many tactics have occasionally succeeded in releasing creative ideas. A fundamental principle is that controlled repression enables the individual to achieve contact with unconscious processes, thereby widening his range of mood and imagery. Without altering the external environment inner changes may be enough to allow new possibilities to be imagined and realized in reality.

Some of the time-honored devices of mankind are connected with alcohol, opium, and other *self-administered* chemicals. The classic story concerns the Persian military commanders who are supposed to have drunk heavily at night and fantasied wildly about battle plans. The next morning action was taken on whatever survived the cold light of hangovers.

Even without the chemical crutch it is feasible to obtain the same result if the group is congenial and willing to encourage and tolerate "brainstorming," or the uttering of uncensored suggestions. This adaptation of the psychoanalytic technique of *free association* is well within the command of any seminar whose members create the appropriate environment for one another.

A seminar group may occasionally agree to explore the creative possibilities of a sensitivity group, or of adopting some other procedure designed to increase the awareness of each participating member of the image that he projects to others. More than free association is involved in sensitivity sessions, since the problem is to discover how A perceives B and how B in turn is perceived by A. This calls for violation of the traditional rules of polite reticence in personal relations. Hence attempts to lead an inexperienced group in this direction may fail, either because the barriers to candid disclosure are too strong, or because the first steps are resented. The participants in the exercise may not agree that the advantages from insight will outweigh the "humiliations" that they must endure from one another. It is by no means certain that the emerging culture of candor will be accepted universally. It may be that plain speaking introduces complications into a limited cooperation group that are better done without. In any case, the decision seminar is free to make up its mind whether to take or leave sensitivity groups.

The influence of a group on creativity cannot be adequately assessed by restricting attention to the manner in which its members respond in the presence of other members. The important insights often come in privacy, sometimes in preparation for group discussion, though often as an aftermath. Members can be encouraged to experiment with *free fantasy* and *meditation* procedures privately.

The policy seminar technique can probably become familiar without putting a stop to inventiveness, since the entire procedure is *self-correction by disciplined experience of context*. By expecting change and taking it for granted that every new detail may provide a clue to a redefined image of the whole, group members are kept alert.

A particular aspect of this process is the *reevaluation of past constructs about the future*. Almost from the first meeting a seminar group can subject itself to the discipline of making specific predictions of future events. And if these predictions include short-term projections, the seminar can benefit by examining the congruence of forecast and occurrence. On the grounds of what inferences were the forecasts made? In the light of subsequent happenings how might the forecasts have been improved? What implications are there for coming events?

It is worth noting that *ego defense* is an important operation for practically everybody, and it may be expedient in a rivalrous world to conduct some decision seminars in ways that put the least strain on delicate ego systems. As suggested before, ego defenses may be too high to permit a seminar to experiment with sensitivity sessions. An example of adaptation is the procedure employed by a group of Wall Street economists who are in competition with one another for important jobs, but who also recognize the advantages of working together within the limits of recognized rules. Each member of the group fills out a schedule answering very specific questions about market fluctuations. It is impossible to "weasel," since the answers are in terms of numerical quotations. A trusted person summarizes the aggregate results and reports them to the group for discussion. The procedure could be extended to the consideration of past forecasts by reporting only the aggregate judgment. (Incidentally, the records of the individual economists are on file and may be released to a specific person if the individual is sufficiently happy with the record.)

Many policy training groups will disdain the ego defenseness of the Wall Street economists and join in candid appraisal of their past estimates. They may also agree to supplement group deliberations by having an occasional analysis of seminar proceedings made by an outside specialist. Sometimes the report may enable a member to become aware of a bias that he may plan to overcome, or at least to take into account. Some participants seem to play a rather stably sanguine or pessimistic role in regard to such matters as the level of employment or the probability of an enlarging or diminishing war. The group as a whole may disclose a characteristic bias. It may be helpful in the long run to examine in detail *the consequences of "insight" statements*. Are they simply disregarded as a result of the tendency to forget or not to "hear" unwelcome comment? Is it possible to identify persons who are, on the contrary, disposed to overreact against their previous role? Do insight exercises decrease the courage with which unconventional views are put forward?

Several procedures can be employed to test *certainty and stability of judgment*. Any discussion serves this purpose to the extent that it allows the participants to formulate their positions in detail. In general the atmosphere of a policy seminar is expected to be that of open *inquiring* minds. A major purpose would be defeated if it were turned into a promotional forum where previously frozen positions are defended to the bitter end. We note that inquiry is not incompatible with differences of opinion or with outspoken, vigorous argument. It is a matter of everyday experience to observe that old and trusted friends may sound like irreconcilable enemies to an eavesdropping stranger who is not sure how to interpret what he hears. The participants may be amusing themselves in mock battle; or they may be dead serious and fully comfortable with conflict without contamination by mutual distrust or disrespect.

As a precaution against the oversights that result from the blandness of too facile agreement, it may be helpful to introduce some version of the ancient practice of appointing a devil's advocate, whose assignment would be to develop the case for alternatives likely to be omitted or excluded from careful consideration. This introduction of adversarial procedure is not intended to dominate the deliberations of the seminar but to act as an occasional challenge to established approaches and thoughtways. The adversarial approach, which is the principal device utilized in the law courts of countries with an English tradition, is an unsatisfactory model for the ordinary conduct of decision seminars, because it diverts *too much attention to stating and applying rules of procedure.* Wherever detailed and explicit rules are supposed to be adhered to by a group, there is need of an umpire to protect the deliberations from being interrupted by controversies over procedure. This is time consuming; but more to the point is the temptation embodied in the adversarial situation to encourage gamesmanship in winning points by fooling or wheedling the umpire-judge-chairman into making decisions of little consequence save to the manipulators who want to come out on top. The attention of the group is channeled into frequent win-lose (zero-sum game) confrontations, and the significant objectives of the undertaking are lost sight of.

Nonetheless a competitive game situation has advantages that can be utilized for seminar purposes. Human beings can be readily mobilized by pitting themselves against one another in a win-lose contest. A seminar group may dissolve occasionally into *simulation exercises* in which the political arena is emulated (whether on a world scale, or in reference to less inclusive communities). Members may be divided into teams to play the role of top decisionmakers in the United States, Soviet Russia, and mainland China, for instance. An assignment may be to imagine the sequence of events if China moves into Nepal. Such a game requires an umpire to take responsibility for "reality" and to decide which moves have what effects.

By this time it is well-established that simulation gaming is an experience that does in fact succeed in evoking the competitive impulses of participants. It is also clear that gaming is a means of conferring a vivid sense of reality of future contingencies. The competitors discover many expectations about the future that they may want to reconsider in the light of their experiences in simulation exercises. The fact that an umpire may disagree with their own estimates of reality is itself a challenging occurrence, and it may or may not lead to a revised view of contingencies.

But simulation gaming has limitations that render it unsatisfactory as a total substitute for seminar procedure. The umpire is the judge; hence it is tempting to study the judge and to learn to manipulate the game in ways that take advantage of his assumptions about reality. When the exercises degenerate into a confrontation of this kind, the familiar consequences of an adversarial procedure manifest themselves. Attention is diverted from realities external to the immediate situations, and one of its principal objectives is frustrated.

If the place of an umpire is taken by the "program" that defines the costs and benefits of different categories of choice, the problem of analyzing the umpire is transferred to the study of the programmer. It is reported, for example, that some simulation exercises have a built-in bias in favor of bold, high-risk choices; hence the player who recognizes this is able to benefit.

Whatever its limitations, a decision seminar can benefit from the shake-up effects of simulation gaming. Predispositions are challenged; and this is a means of uncovering previously unrecognized expectations, demands, and identifications.

The most obvious way to alter the predispositions of a group is to change its *social and personality composition.* If the decision seminar movement brings about global seminar networks, it will be possible to use them for the purpose of examining in a systematic and relatively intensive manner the significance for the policy process of the various predispositions distributed about the world. This may become one of the important institutions for conducting a continuing *self-survey of global dispositions* to act for man or for various subdivisions of mankind.

It is not difficult to enumerate many factors that can usefully affect the choice of personnel in decision seminars. Assuming the same field of specialization for a moment, it is evident that predispositions are affected by length of exposure to the specialty (roughly measured by age), type of methodological training (e.g., mathematico-statistical, historical and comparative, philosophical, legalistic), and category of professional activity (e.g., teaching, research, consultation, administration); as well as by affiliation with or exposure to various cultures (e.g., national, ethnic), social classes (elite, mid-elite, the rank and file of transnational, national, subnational power, enlightenment, wealth, well-being, affection, respect, rectitude), interest groups (less than class or interclass), and personality groups (value priorities, mechanisms). The same variables are pertinent to every specialty, and the specialties in varying proportion will affect results.

It is relevant for a working group to catalog the many hypotheses that are open to confirmation (or disconfirmation) in reference to the functioning of decision seminars of varying composition. In general, it will probably be found that the greater the heterogeneity, the longer the time required for detailed mutual understanding. The most significant variables appear to be those that affect value commitments for or against human dignity, expectations of an indulgent or deprivational future for one's preferences, self-confidence and creative imagination in devising strategies to optimalize purposes. Commitment to human dignity appears to depend in high degree on indoctrination in a cultural setting where this is the prevailing ideology. It is traditional to expect the young to exhibit a wider spectrum of social attitudes than is characteristic of the older generation.

Seminar Diffusion

The future of decision seminars as an instructional technique depends on the experience of those who try it. Hence it is important to consider the expected and realized value pay-offs that participants receive. In a training environment the teachers and the taught must perceive that they are relatively better off by spending time in decision seminars than by engaging in other training exercises. The point is not that this particular device will or ought to monopolize the instructional program. Rather, the inference is that its relative place will ultimately depend on its perceived relationship to alternative exercises.

Presumably the principal aim of policy training is to contribute to the skill and enlightenment of all concerned. We have mentioned many pertinent skills, such as the projection of future events and the continuing critique of forecasts in the light of occurrences. Reference has also been made to the cultivation of creativity by inventing realistic policy objectives and strategies. A complete inventory of skills would include some of the capabilities more commonly utilized in conventional training, such as the handling of historical sources, the formation of sophisticated scientific theories (models, hypotheses), the conduct of interviews, and other procedures of data gathering and processing. Each identifiable skill is appropriate to the expansion of knowledge *of* and *in* decision processes. Of particular concern to our instructional aims is enlightenment, a value outcome that goes beyond the bits of knowledge essential to any specific skill. Enlightenment goes beyond skill in the sense that it is contextual. To be enlightened about man and society is to be in command of an explicit map of the whole.

It is, of course, impossible for anyone to escape an *implicit* map of the self-in-context. But the cognitive map is rarely brought deliberately or fully into the open unless the individual is exposed to an instructional experience that rewards him by bringing the implicit image of reality to the full focus of waking awareness. This is the sense in which policy training operations are designed to influence the content made available at the focus of attention and to adopt the procedures effectively adapted to the task. The enlightened person is aware of his assumptions about the past, present, and future of himself, his cultural environment, and his natural environment. Our recommended goal is to provide undogmatic access to inclusive versions of reality, so that the chances are increased that the individual will use his own capabilities of imagination and judgment.

The policy science emphasis is itself in continual tension with tendencies to distintegrate the contextual orientation on behalf of a bundle of skills that can be objectively identified and tested. The policy science approach does not neglect or dispraise skill. On the contrary it encourages and integrates skill, and provides a built-in challenge to the invention of new and improved operational capabilities.

The fundamental strategy of the decision seminar device is to subordinate detail to context, and to do so, not by neglecting detail, but by subjecting each detail to the discipline of the relevant reality, which is the ever-unfolding map of the future. The map of the future is perceived, not as an instrument of the "inevitable," but as a tool of guided innovation and optimum change. The procedures employed in organizing the focus of attention in a contextual seminar are among the most direct means of contributing to the potential policy analyst and policy operator in every sector of public and civic order.

The tactics of an instructional program must be adapted to the predispositions of those who enter into it—hence the flexibility implied in the scope of particular seminars (such as counterparts of structure, function, or problem), as well as the use of such auxiliary aids as audio-visual material, or the management of sensitivity, adversarial, simulation, and other means of enriching the experience.

Participants will become more confident of the benefits when decision seminar technique spreads to official and unofficial organizations. Many transitional arrangements will expedite diffusion, such as bringing some officials directly into seminars to function as full members. Many detailed problems arise in this connection, such as the confidentiality of official material. But these questions are not new, and have been met many times by officials who work with private consultants or engage to some extent in private teaching or research.

As decision seminars spread, it becomes feasible for networks of such seminars to parallel their strategies and hence to exemplify a *strategy of simultaneity* in seeking to accomplish results.

Decision seminars are likely to be carried forward by policy scientists who take them for granted as the most appropriate means of conducting the intelligence and appraisal function for organizations and for individual decisionmakers.

Simultaneously, the technique will be carried backwards through the preprofessional stages of training until the concept of self-in-context will be implemented from the beginning to the end of life with due regard to the capacity of the developing human being for creative and continuing participation in the life of tomorrow.

Supplementary Laboratories

The comprehensive character of the decision seminar technique does not exhaust the training techniques adapted to policy science training. In the preceding discussion, reference was made to the possibility of incorporating in the agenda of a specific seminar procedures that would shake up established routines and contribute to creativity. Some of these practices may be most effective when they are briefly included in the program of the whole group. We also referred to the possibility that while the general seminar might benefit from individual exposure to a given training opportunity, the objectives of the total operation would suffer if the training were not obtained separately.

The rapid multiplication of training techniques renders it feasible for policy science schools and programs to arrange for supplementary laboratories to provide facilities for each individual or small group when motivations are high, and when deficiencies have been discovered. Modern instructional devices can be adapted to such supplementary purposes as enabling the student to overcome deficiencies of preparation in logic, mathematics, statistics, computer programming, interviewing, spectator-recording, and so on.

Among the techniques that can be learned in individual and small group laboratories are self-observation and analysis. It is not enough to know where one stands in terms of test performance on aptitude or temperament. The significant problem is to consider alternative interpretations of the results, and the devising of programs in some cases designed to modify personality dispositions and levels of operation. Behavioral tests are seldom to be taken as establishing limits within which no deliberate change is possible. They are chiefly useful in clarifying the present predispositions, and in directing attention to the probable costs (in terms of time and other assets) of bringing about a given level of change.

Among supplementary laboratory programs, *insight* training is particularly important for the policy scientist, since he needs to assess his own role, as a conditioning factor in any number of situations. We referred to some of the methods that have been developed in recent decades, such as sensitivity training and self-observation under the influence of various chemicals. Traditional psychoanalysis laid so much emphasis on the "deeper" motivations that it failed to provide for proportionate, contextual insight into social reality at different levels. Individuals were trained to associate freely in order to learn more about themselves by permitting hitherto suppressed or repressed impulses to achieve full expression at the focus of waking attention. The individual was trained to endure the anxieties involved, and also to consider interpretations or explanatory theories of why he possesses such impulses, and why they seem particularly active at the moment.

The technique is being adapted to reality critique by allowing the individual to become more aware of his relationship to the various value-institution contexts to which he is currently exposed, and to which he has been exposed (with many value-indulgent or value-deprivational results) in the past. For instance, it is often more disconcerting for students to examine the degree to which they have been given and have received indulgences or deprivations in terms of respect, enlightenment, and power than in more conventional categories of love or sexuality. Similarly, the significance of the public language of political, economic, and other myths changes when the private meanings of these myths are brought systematically into the open. For example, private business (capitalism) may be perceived of young people who have been reared in opulent families as corrupt and arrogant by a substantial percentage. The corresponding group in large socialist countries may have come to stigmatize the *bureaucrats* and the *political police* in the same way.

As well as programs of policy analysis and development, *personal logs* are among the technical procedures that can contribute to a lifetime of self-appraisal. These logs combine essay statements with quantitative recording. In simplest form such a log is a time record of interaction with others. For scientific purposes the technique can provide data about how those who function in position x in a given organization actively relate to coordinate position holders, to superiors, and to subordinates, and how the formal lines of authority are supplemented by informal contact. Although the scientific results of contact studies need not be negligible, they are probably much more important as means of introducing a self-correcting factor into tendencies toward restrictive, self-segregating association.

By participating in field work during training years, the policy scientist can become aware from the earliest time of the difficult and changing lines that practically reconcile the obligation of the profession to contribute to published knowledge and the obligation to protect the integrity of decision processes.

Extreme situations rarely present difficulties. No serious person would disseminate observations made by permission and with an agreement that time must elapse before scholarly or general publication takes place. The continuing seminar technique is well adapted to confront students, faculty, and practitioners with the complexities involved in prescribing and giving effect to norms of conduct that cover the range of action open to those who provide professional services for clients, and who also have the obligation to play an active and fully responsible role in public and civic order.

Through coming years the institutions of professional preparation, client service, and direct participation will undergo the transformations required by the dynamism of a world dependent on science-based technology, and under perpetual challenge to adjust prevailing value priorities, levels of value accumulation and enjoyment to the opportunities and dangers involved. A contextual, problem-oriented, multi-method approach to public and civic order can be expected to improve our knowledge *of* and *in* decision processes, and to contribute to expertness in the formulation of policy in terms of realizable objectives and strategies. Such at least is the aspiration of the emerging policy sciences.

Bibliographic Notes

Chapter 1

An important interpretation of the policy science field, joined with a valuable bibliographic guide, is in Yehezkel Dror, *Public Policy Re-examined* (San Francisco: Chandler, 1968). The term was introduced in Harold D. Lasswell, "The Policy Orientation," in *The Policy Sciences: Recent Developments in Scope and Methods,* eds. Daniel Lerner and Harold D. Lasswell (Stanford: Stanford University Press, 1951). See Harold D. Lasswell, "Policy Sciences," *International Encyclopedia of the Social Sciences,* Vol. 12 (1968), also Robert S. Lynd, *Knowledge for What?* (Princeton: Princeton University Press, 1948).

On the emergence of civilization consult V. Gordon Childe, *What Happened in History?* (Baltimore: Pelican Books, 1954).

On ideological systems and their specialized users read Mario A. Levi, *Political Power in the Ancient World* (New York: New American Library, 1965); Eric A. Havelock, *The Liberal Temper in Greek Politics* (New Haven: Yale University Press, 1957); D. S. Nivison and A. F. Wright, eds., *Confucianism in Action* (Stanford: Stanford University Press, 1959); and V. P. Varma, *Hindu Political Thought and Its Metaphysical Foundations,* 2nd ed. (Banares: Motilal Banarsidass, 1959).

An autobiography that contains many clues to the expanding role of a contemporary scientist-engineer in public policy is Vannevar Bush, *Pieces of the Action* (New York: William Morrow, 1970).

Chapter 2

The social process and decision models employed here were outlined in Harold D. Lasswell and Abraham Kaplan, *Power and Society* (New Haven: Yale University Press, 1950; paperback, 19), and partially exemplified in the study of law, as in M. S. McDougal, H. D. Lasswell, and I. A. Vlasic, *Law and Public Order in Space* (New Haven: Yale University Press, 1963), and in other sectors of society, as indicated in Arnold A. Rogow, Jr., *Politics, Personality and Social Science in the Twentieth Century* (Chicago: University of Chicago Press, 1969). For further information, read Harold D. Lasswell and Allan R. Holmberg, "Toward a General Theory of Directed Value Accumulation and Institutional Development," in *Political and Administrative Development,* ed. Ralph Braibanti (Durham, N.C.: Duke University Press, 1969).

For a comprehensive approach see Amitai Etzioni, *The Active Society* (New York: Free Press of Glencoe, 1968); Raymond A. Bauer, *Social Indicators* (Cambridge: M.I.T. Press, 1966); and Bertram M. Gross, *The State of the Nation : Social-System Accounting* (London: Tavistock, 1966).

Representative of studies that link contextual models in particular value-institution areas with operational indices and with policy are B. M. Russett, H. R. Alker, Jr., K. W. Deutsch, and H. D. Lasswell, *World Handbook of Political and Social Indicators* (New Haven: Yale University Press, 1964); H. E. Klarman, *The Economics of Health* (New York: Columbia University Press, 1965); Samuel Bowles, *Planning Systems for Educational Growth* (Cambridge: Harvard University Press, 1969); A. J. Reiss, O. D. Duncan, P. K. Hatt, and C. C. North, *Occupations and Social Status* (New York: Free Press of Glencoe, 1962); Frank G. Dickinson, *The Changing Position of Philanthropy in the American Economy* (New York: Columbia University Press, 1970); Fritz Machlup, *The Production and Distribution of Knowledge in the United States* (Princeton: Princeton University Press, 1962); and Lawrence Klein, et al., *The Brookings Quarterly Econometric Model of the United States* (Chicago: Rand McNally, 1965).

Much of urban and regional planning literature utilizes a wide range of value indicators: Walter Isard, *General Theory: Social, Political, Economic, and Regional with Particular Reference to Decision-making Analysis* (Cambridge: M.I.T. Press, 1969).

Chapter 3

On the problem of clarifying values a compendious statement is in Arnold Brecht, *Political Theory* (Princeton: Princeton University Press, 1959). Efforts to ground or to specify preferred goals are found in Carl J. Friedrich, ed., *The Public Interest* (New York: Atherton Press, 1962). Current discussion can be followed in the journals *Ethics* (University of Chicago) and *Inquiry* (initiated by Arne Naess at the University of Oslo).

For a description of past trends and situations read Hans Meyerhoff, ed., *The Philosophy of History in Our Time* (New York: Harper, 1959); H. J. Muller, *The Uses of the Past* (New York: Oxford, University Press 1952); and J. H. Plumb, *Death of the Past* (Boston: Houghton Mifflin, 1970).

Concerning scientific explanation and procedure consult T. S. Kuhn, *The Structure of Scientific Revolutions* (Chicago: University of Chicago Press, 1962); Ernest Nagel, *The Structure of Science: Problems in the Logic of Scientific Explanation* (New York: Harcourt, Brace and World, 1961); and Abraham Kaplan, *The Conduct of Inquiry* (San Francisco: Chandler, 1964).

Material on projection can be found in Bertrand de Jouvenel, *The Art of Con-*

jecture (New York: Basic Books, 1967); Dennis Gabor, *Inventing the Future* (New York: Lechner & Warburg, 1963); and Daniel Bell, "Twelve Modes of Prediction," in *Penguin Survey of the Social Sciences,* ed. Julius Gould (Middlesex, Eng.: Penguin, 1965).

On policy alternatives, a simplified statement is in Irvin D. J. Bross, *Design for Decision* (New York: Macmillan, 1953). More complex is C. West Churchman, *Prediction and Optimal Decision* (Englewood Cliffs, N.J.: Prentice-Hall, 1961). The measuring and aggregation of values are analyzed in Kenneth J. Arrow, *Social Choice and Individual Values,* 2nd ed. (New York: John Wiley, 1963) and in Jerome Rothenberg, *The Measurement of Social Welfare* (Englewood Cliffs, N. J.; Prentice-Hall, 1961). The challenge to create integrative rather than compromise solutions is in H. Metcalf and L. Urwich, eds., *Dynamic Administration: The Collected Papers of Mary Parker Follett* (New York: Harper, n.d.). On models for scientific explanation and policy purposes see Karl W. Deutsch, *The Nerves of Government: Models of Political Communication and Control,* 2nd ed. (New York: Free Press of Glencoe, 1966), and Herbert A. Simon and Allen Newell, "Models: Their Uses and Limitations," in *The State of the Social Sciences,* ed. Leonard D. White (Chicago: The University of Chicago, 1956).

Chapter 4

All constructs of the past-present-future context rely in some degree on extrapolating trends, although these require reconciliation when they imply future contradiction. See Herman Kahn, *On Escalation: Metaphors and Scenarios* (New York: Praeger, 1965). Olaf Helmer's "delphi technique" systematically interrogates specialists about their future expectations; see *Social Technology* (New Haven: Yale University Press, 1964). See also Erich Jantsch, *Technological Forecasting in Perspective* (Paris: OECD, Working Document DAS/SPR/66,12,1966) and William F. Butler and Robert A. Karesh, *How Business Economists Forecast* (Englewood Cliffs, N.J.: Prentice-Hall, 1966).

Combining projections with methodological comment is John McHale, *The Future of the Future* (New York: Braziller, 1969); "Toward the Year 2000: Work in Progress," *Daedalus* (Summer 1967); Robert Jungk and John Galtung, eds., *Mankind 2000* (Oslo: Norwegian University Press, 1968); and Herman Kahn and A. J. Wiener, *The Year 2000* (New York: Macmillan, 1967).

The use of a conceptual map to analyze and guide social change is referred to in connection with the Cornell Project in Peru by Allen Holmberg in "Experimental Intervention in a Field Situation," *Human Organization* 14 (1955): 23–26. A partial exemplification of prototyping is Robert Rubenstein and Harold D. Lasswell, *The Sharing of Power in a Psychiatric Hospital* (New Haven: Yale University Press, 1966). Movement in this direction is indicated in George

F. Fairweather, *Methods for Experimental Social Innovation* (New York: John Wiley, 1968).

Some technical procedures for policy or management analysis are found in Arthur D. Hall, *A Methodology for Systems Engineering* (Princeton: Van Nostrand, 1962); F. Paul Degormo, *Engineering Economy,* 3rd ed. (New York: Macmillan, 1965); David Novick, ed., *Program Budgeting: Program Analysis and the Federal Government* (Cambridge: Harvard University Press, 1965); Edward F. R. Hearle and Raymond J. Mason, *A Data-Processing System for State and Local Governments* (Englewood Cliffs, N.J.: Prentice-Hall, 1963); Leonard W. Hein, *The Quantitative Approach to Management Decision* (Englewood Cliffs, N.J.: Prentice-Hall, 1967); John A. Postley, *Computers and People* (New York: McGraw-Hill, 1960); Edward C. Bursk and John F. Chapman, eds., *New Decision Making Tools for Managers* (Cambridge: Harvard University Press, 1963); J. W. Forrester, *Industrial Dynamics* (Cambridge: M.I.T. Press, 1961); Garry Brewer, "Mastering the Complexity of Urban Decision" (Ph.D. dissertation, Yale University, 1970); and Ronald D. Brunner and Garry D. Brewer, *Organized Complexity: Empirical Theories of Political Development,* (New York: Free Press, 1971).

Chapter 5

Intelligence: Criteria for appraising the performance of public information systems are proposed in *A Free and Responsible Press* (by the Commission on Freedom of the Press, Chicago: University of Chicago Press, 1947). Suggestions for evaluating the credibility of intelligence estimates based on content analysis are given by Alexander F. George, *Propaganda Analysis: A Study of Inferences Made from Nazi War Propaganda in World War II* (Evanston: Row, Peterson, 1959). On "Roots of Intelligence Failure" see the summary chart in H. L. Wilensky, *Organizational Intelligence: Knowledge and Policy in Government and Industry* (New York: Basic Books, 1967), pp. 175–78; for further material read Roger Hilsman, *Strategic Intelligence and National Decisions* (Glencoe, Ill.: Free Press, 1956); Harry H. Ransom, *Central Intelligence and National Security* (Cambridge: Harvard University Press, 1958); and Washington Platt, *Strategic Intelligence Production: Basic Principles* (New York: Praeger, 1957). On planning consult Martin Meyerson and E. C. Banfield, *Politics, Planning and the Public Interest* (Glencoe, Ill.: Free Press, 1955).

Promotion: Hierarchical organizations often have no differentiated agency for the promotion of internal policy. They may, however, have specialized instruments to affect the policy processes of the larger arena in which they operate. In a dispersed organization top officials must emphasize promotion. See, for instance, Elmer E. Cornwell, Jr., *Presidential Leadership of Public Opinion* (Bloomington, Ind.: Indiana University Press, 1965). Concerning implicit of explicit criteria for parties and pressure groups, see R. Joseph Monson, Jr., and Mark W. Cannon, *The Makers of Public Policy: American Power Groups and Their Ideologies* with James Deakin, *The Lobbyist* (Washington, D.C.: Public Affairs Press, 1966); and Donald R. Hall, *Cooperative Lobbying—The Power of Pressure* (Tucson, Ariz.: University of Arizona Press, 1969). The specialists on public relations who manage intelligence for persuasive purposes present policy problems.

Prescription: When "conventional" prescriptions, such as statutes and administrative regulations, are examined, they may turn out to be symbolic gestures more important for such promotional effects as catharsis than for true prescriptions. The point is developed in Murray Edelman, *The Symbolic Uses of Politics* (Urbana, Ill.: University of Illinois Press, 1964). An examination of the process of norm crystallization, hence of criteria for its assessment, is in Wesley L. Gould and Michael Barkun, *International Law and the Social Sciences,* especially chapter 5 (Princeton: Princeton University Press, 1970). Consult also Louis H. Mayo and Ernest M. Jones, "Legal Policy Decision Process," *George Washington Law Review* 33 (1964):318–456. The budgetary allocation of resources to policy objectives is a principal component of prescribing. Criteria specify acceptable balances between inputs and outputs for current operations, and for capital formation and withdrawals; and call for evidence pertinent to estimates of net advantage. See Aaron Wildavsky, *The Politics of the Budgetary Process* (Boston: Little, Brown, 1964).

Invocation: Although the police function is to make a provisional application of prescriptions to concrete factual circumstances, the conventionally designated police often perform other functions as well, especially application. See Joseph Goldstein, "Police Discretion Not to Involve the Criminal Process: Law Visibility Decisions in the Administration of Criminal Law," *Yale Law Journal* 69 (1960):543–94; and Jerome H. Skolnick, *Justice without Trial* (New York: John Wiley, 1966). The Swedish ombudsman deals with claims that go beyond explicit legal prescription. See Donald C. Rowat, ed., *The Ombudsman: Citizen's Defender* (London: George Allen & Unwin, 1965).

Application: The literature of bureaucracy and large-scale organization abounds in explicit and implicit criteria of appraisal. Consult Bertram M. Gross, *The Managing of Organizations* (New York: Free Press of Glencoe, 1964); Herbert A. Simon, *Administrative Behavior: A Study of Decision Making Processes in Administrative Organizations,* 2nd ed. (New York: Macmillan, 1957); Peter M. Blau, *The Dynamics of Bureaucracy,* 2nd rev. ed. (Chicago: University of Chicago Press, 1963); and Anthony Downs, *Inside Bureaucracy* (Boston: Little, Brown, 1967), especially the summary of hypotheses on pp. 261–280. Suggestive limited studies include Chris Argyris, *Some Causes of Organizational Ineffectiveness within the Department of State* (Washington, D.C.: Department of State, 1967); William W. Kaufman, *The McNamara Strategy* (New York:

Harper, 1964); and Hans Zeisel and Harry Kalven, Jr., *Delay in the Courts* (Boston: Little, Brown, 1959).

Termination: The legal doctrines invoked in controversies over the magnitude of the compensation appropriate to the taking of property for public purposes provide criteria for evaluating the structures involved. However, the studies of expropriation presently available are inadequate, since as a rule they are designed to serve the purposes of a particular party.

Appraisal: Some legislative and executive commissions are relatively limited to the intelligence function (e.g., to initiate inquiry to establish facts), promotion (to try to win support for a predetermined policy), prescription (to negotiate an arrangement to be subsequently rubber-stamped by a conventional authority), invocation (to initiate action in concrete cases), or application or termination (to take final action, including disposition of claims under previous prescriptions). Some commissions are chiefly limited to appraisal, since they characterize aggregate trends and propose explanations or targets of responsibility. See Thomas E. Cronin and Sanford D. Greenberg, eds., *The Presidential Advisory System* (New York: Harper, 1969); Charles J. Hanser, *Guide to Decision, The Royal Commission* (Totowa, N.J.: Bedminster Press, 1965); and Jack Stieber, Walter E. Oberer, Michael Harrington, *Democracy and Public Review: An Analysis of the UAW Public Review Board* (Santa Barbara: Center for the Study of Democratic Institutions, 1960).

Inclusive: Among studies concerned with criteria of general relevance, though oriented toward particular tasks, are Robert E. Kuenne, *The Polaris Missile Strike: A General Economic Systems Analysis* (Columbus; Ohio State University Press, 1966) and Joseph Borkin, *The Corrupt Judge* (New York: Clarkson N. Potter, 1962). On the interplay among decision agencies see Lawrence H. Chamberlain, *The President, Congress and Legislation* (New York: Columbia University Press, 1946).

Chapter 6

The allocation of authority and control among the organized and unorganized, individual and group participants in a given context is the *constitutive* process. It is concerned, not with management within a system, but with structure protection or alteration. Much organizational theory is pertinent to the policy problems of the constitutive process. See, for instance, relevant discussions in James G. March, *Handbook of Organizations* (Chicago: Rand McNally, 1965) and M. S. McDougal, H. D. Lasswell, and W. M. Reisman, "The World Constitutive Process of Authoritative Decision," *Journal of Legal Education* 19 (1967): 253–300, 403–37. The traditional wisdom found in political theory is summarized in Carl J. Friedrich, *Man and His Government* (New York: McGraw-Hill, 1963). The literature on developmental and comparative studies is the richest in

cross-cultural detail and in the overt or latent formulation of experience perti-
nent to an overriding policy goal: for example, Lucian W. Pye, ed., *Communica-
tions and Political Development* (Princeton: Princeton University Press, 1963);
Joseph LaPalombara and Myron Weiner, eds., *Political Parties and Political De-
velopment* (Princeton: Princeton University Press, 1966); Stein Rokkan with
Angus Campbell, Per Torsvik, and Henry Valen, *Citizens, Elections, Parties*
(Oslo: Universitets laget, 1970); Sven Groennings, E. W. Kelly, and Michael
Leiserson, eds., *The Study of Coalition Behavior* (New York: Holt, Rinehart &
Winston, 1970); Ralph Braibanti, ed., *Political and Administrative Development*
(Durham, N.C.: Duke University Press, 1969); John J. Johnson, ed., *The Role
of the Military in Underdeveloped Countries* (Princeton: Princeton University
Press, 1962); Glendon Schubert and David J. Danelski, *Comparative Judicial
Behavior* (New York: Oxford University Press, 1969); and Paul Diesing, *Rea-
son in Society: Five Types of Decision and Their Social Conditions* (Urbana:
University of Illinois Press, 1962).

Chapter 7

The actual and potential roles of policy scientists are indicated in studies such as
Robert Gilpin and Christopher Wright, eds., *Scientists and National Policy Mak-
ing* (New York: Columbia University Press, 1964); Don K. Price, *The Scien-
tific Estate* (Cambridge: Harvard University Press, 1965); Klaus Lompe,
Wissonschäftliche Beratung der Politik [Scientific Consultation in Politics]
(Gottingen: Otto Schwartz, 1966); C. P. Snow, *Science and Government,* rev.
with new appendix (New York: New American Library, 1962); Edward S.
Flash, Jr., *Economic Advice and Presidential Leadership* (New York: Columbia
University Press, 1965); Morris Janowitz, *The New Military* (New York: Rus-
sell Sage Foundation, 1964); Bruce L. R. Smith, *The RAND Corporation: Case
Study of a Non-Profit Advisory Corporation* (Cambridge: Harvard University
Press, 1966); Harvey Brooks, *The Government of Science* (Cambridge: M.I.T.
Press, 1968); Harold Wool, *The Military Specialist* (Baltimore: Johns Hopkins
Press, 1968); R. Hofstader and W. P. Metzger, *The Development of Academic
Freedom in the United States* (New York: Columbia University Press, 1955);
T. Caplow and P. J. McGee, *The Academic Marketplace* (New York: Basic
Books, 1958); L. Wilson, *The Academic Man* (New York: Oxford University
Press, 1942); Boyd R. Keenan, ed., *Science and the University* (Chicago: Uni-
versity of Chicago Press, 1962); Donald A. Strickland, *Scientists in Politics:
1945–1946* (Lafayette, Ind.: Purdue University Studies, 1968); Eugene B. Skol-
nikoff, *Science, Technology and American Foreign Policy* (Cambridge: M.I.T.
Press, 1967); "Lawyers in Developing Societies," *Law and Society Review* 3
(1968–69): entire issue; Charles Horsky, *The Washington Lawyer* (Boston: Lit-

tle, Brown, 1952); David R. Deener, *The Attorneys General and International Law* (The Hague: Nijhoff, 1957); Jerome E. Carlin, *Lawyers on Their Own* (New Brunswick: Rutgers University Press, 1962); Erwin O. Smigel, *The Wall Street Lawyer* (New York: Free Press of Glencoe, 1964); Walter O. Weyrauch, *The Personality of Lawyers* (New Haven: Yale University Press, 1964); Harold K. Jacobson and Eric Stein, *Diplomats, Scientists and Politicians: The United States and the Nuclear Test Ban Negotiations* (Ann Arbor: University of Michigan Press, 1966); "The Professions," *Daedalus* 92 (1963): entire issue; and Harold D. Lasswell, "Must Science Serve Political Power?" *American Psychologist* 25 (1970): 117–23.

Surveys: A Survey of the Behavioral and Social Sciences was published under the auspices of the Committee on Science and Public Policy of the National Academy of Sciences and the Problems and Policy Committee of the Social Science Research Council. A general volume is *The Behavioral and Social Sciences: Outlook and Needs* (Englewood Cliffs, N.J.: Prentice-Hall, 1969). Separate volumes are to be found under the appropriate discipline. See especially Nancy Ruggles, ed., *Economics* (Englewood Cliffs, N.J.: Prentice-Hall, 1970); also, *The Behavioral Sciences and the Federal Government* (Washington, D.C.: National Academy of Sciences, 1968); and Gene M. Lyons, *The Uneasy Partnership: Social Science and the Federal Government in the Twentieth Century* (New York: Russell Sage Foundation, 1969).

Chapter 8

Training programs require exposure to contextual concepts, problem orientations, and methods of obtaining, processing, and utilizing data. Representative titles (in addition to previous citations) include H. D. Lasswell and M. S. McDougal, "Legal Education and Public Policy: Professional Training in the Public Interest," *Yale Law Journal* 52 (1943): 203–95, and H. D. Lasswell, *The Future of Political Science* (New York: Atherton Press, 1963).

The Policy Sciences magazine has arranged for two special issues on the teaching of policy sciences at universities (special issue editor, Yehezkel Dror). Included is a discussion by H. D. Lasswell of "The Continuing Seminar as an instrument of Policy Science Instruction."

See also James A. Robinson, "Participant Observation, Political Interneship and Research," *Political Science Annual* 2 (1969): 71–110; George F. Fairweather, *Methods for Experimental Social Innovation* (New York: John Wiley, 1968); George Gerbner, Ole R. Holsti, Klaus Krippendorff, William J. Paisley, and Philip J. Stone, *The Analysis of Communication Content: Developments in Scientific Theories and Computer Techniques* (New York: John Wiley, 1969) Ward Edwards and Amos Tversky, eds., *Decision Making* (Middlesex, Eng.:

Penguin, 1967); Barry Collins and Harold Guetzkow, *A Social Psychology of Group Processes for Decision Making* (New York: John Wiley, 1964); Nelson N. Foote, ed., *Household Decisionmaking* (New York: New York University Press, 1961); David Braybrooke and Charles E. Lindblom, *Strategy of Decision* (New York: Free Press of Glencoe, 1963); Harold D. Anderson, ed., *Creativity and Its Cultivation* (New York: Harper, 1959); Alex F. Osborn, *Applied Imagination,* rev. ed. (New York: Scribner's, 1957); and Donald W. Taylor, Paul C. Berry, and Clifton H. Block, ". . .brainstorming. . .," *Administrative Science Quarterly* 3 (1958): 23 pp.

For further study, read M. Blalock, Jr., *Causal Inferences in Nonexperimental Research* (Chapel Hill, N.C.: University of North Carolina Press, 1964); James S. Coleman, *Introduction to Mathematical Sociology* (New York: Free Press, 1964); Davis B. Bobrow and Judah L. Schwartz, eds., *Computers and the Policy-Making Community* (Englewood Cliffs, N.J.: Prentice-Hall, 1968); Ithiel deSola Pool, Robert P. Abelson, and Samuel Popkin, *Candidates, Issues and Strategies* (Cambridge: M.I.T. Press, 1962); Guy H. Orcutt, Martin Greenberger, John Korbel, and Alice M. Rivlin, *Microanalysis of Socioeconomic Systems: A Simulation Study* (New York: Harper, 1961); John P. Crecine, *Governmental Problem Solving* (Chicago: Rand McNally, 1969); Geoffrey P. S. Clarkson, *Portfolio Selection: A Simulation of Investment Trust* (Englewood Cliffs, N.J.: Prentice-Hall, 1962); Edward A. Suchman, *Evaluation Research: Principles and Practices in Public Service and Social Action Programs* (New York: Russell Sage Foundation, 1967); Harold D. Lasswell, "Toward a Continuing Appraisal of the Impact of Law on Society," *Rutgers Law Review* 21 (1967): 645–77; and Herbert J. Gans, *People and Plans* (New York: Free Press, 1968).

The Phases of Optimal Public Policymaking

Condensed from Yehezkel Dror, *Public Policymaking Re-examined*
(San Francisco: Chandler, 1968)

Metapolicymaking stage

1. Processing values (specifying and ordering relevant values)

2. Processing reality (perceiving pertinent features of past and future)

3. Processing problems (statement in action oriented form)

4. Surveying, processing and developing resources

5. Designing, evaluating and redesigning the policy making system

6. Allocating problems, values, and resources

7. Determining policymaking strategy

Policymaking stage

8. Suballocating resources

9. Establishing operational goals, with some order of priority for them

10. Establishing a set of other, major significant values, with some order of priority for them (identifying other relevant values likely to become involved)

11. Preparing a set of major alternatives, including some "good" ones

12. Preparing a set of reliable predictions of the significant benefits and costs of the various alternatives.

13. Comparing the predicted benefits and costs of the alternatives, and identifying the best ones.

14. Evaluating the benefits and costs of the "best" alternative and deciding whether it is "good" or not

Post Policymaking Stage

15. Motivating the executing policy

16. Executing the policy

17. Evaluating the policy after executing it

Feedback Stages

18. Communication and feedback channels multiply, interconnecting all phases

Index

Act, defined, 16
Affection value, 42
Alternatives, as
  problem orientation, 55ff
Application outcome, 29
  criteria of function, 92
Appraisal outcome, 29
  role of policy scientist, 59
  of ordinary policy process, 76ff
  of policy impacts, 76
  criteria of function, 93
  varying levels of analysis, 95ff
Arenas of power, 30
  inclusive and comprehensive, 36
Aristotle 10
Attention and sleep, 61
  autism, 61
  selective inattention, 61
  obsessive preoccupation, 62
Authority, 27
  formulated authority and control, 98ff

Base values, 3, 26
Benton, William B., xii
Brewer, Gary, 73
Brunner, Ronald, 73

Careers in policy sciences, 4, 131
Centralization-decentralization, 31
Civic order, 1
Civilization, 9
Clients of policy scientists, 76ff
Collaborative strategies, 26
Communicative strategies, 26
Complementary interests, problem of, 81ff
Concentration-deconcentration, 31
Conditions, as problem orientation, 49

as equilibrium, 50
  cyclical, 51
Confucius, 10
Consequences, aggregate and particular, 12
Constitutive process appraisal, 98ff
  goals and principles, 100ff
  clarifying and giving effect to common interests, 105ff
  model for analysis, of special and common interests, 106
  model for regulatory activities, 109
Content, principles of, 14, 39
Contexuality, 3
  contextual mapping, 63ff
Control, 27
Conventional relevance, 2, 14ff
Core periodicals, 114
Counterpart seminars, 66
Criteria of policy, 85ff
  for the intelligence function, 86
  for the promotional function, 88
  for the prescribing function, 90
  for the invoking function, 91
  for application, 92
  for termination, 92
    of the appraisal function, 93
    of all functions and structures, 94

Decision process model, 27
Decision seminars,
  continuing, 142
  requirements and procedures, 144
  diffusion, 155
Definition,
  policy sciences, 1
Developmental constructs,
  as method, 67ff
  distinguished from Marxist model, 67
Dewey, John, xii

Diplomacy, 26
Diversity, 4, 58ff
Doctrines, as norms of conduct, 41
    as transempirical propositions, 41
Dror, Yehezkel, xii

Economic strategy, 26
Enlightenment value, 42
Expectations, of power, 52

Feynman, Richard, G., 3
Functional relevance, 2

Goals, 40ff

Hammurabi, 10
Hoffman, Paul G., xii

Identity, professional, 112ff
    developing a distinctive, 120
Incorporating computer simulation, 72ff
    correlational, formal deductive and
        computer modelling, 73
Institutions, defined, 22
Intelligence outcome, 28
    criteria for the function, 86ff
    knowledge network, 112
Invocation outcome, 29
Interaction, defined, 14
Integrative training of policy scientists,
    137
    uses of a prospectus, 140
    study and field experience, 141
    diverse problem emphasis, 141
    personal and situational contexts, 142
    continuing decision seminars, 142ff

Kautilya, 10
Knowledge network, 112ff
    inner structure of knowledge institu-
        tions, 123

Lerner, Daniel, xii
Lifton, Robert J., 149

Maximization postulate, 16
McDougal, Myres S., xii
Merriam, Charles E., xii
Military strategy, 26
Myth, including doctrine, formula, mi-
    randa, 24, 25

Nation states, as
    unitary, 31
    federal, 32

Occupations, defined, 12
Outcomes, defined, 17
    gross and net, 20

Participant observer standpoint, 74ff
Participants, in social process, 24
Participation, encouragement of con-
        tinuous general, 117
    bureaucratism, 119
Perspectives, of identity, demand,
        expectation, 24
Planning, or ordinary policy process, 77
    impact, 77, 97
    constitutive, 77, 98ff
Plato, 10
Policy process, ordinary, 76ff
Policy and science, 2
Power, as lawful, naked, pretended, 27
    as authority and control, 27
Power values, 42
    shared power as goal, 44ff
    conditions, 52
Prescription outcome, 29
    criteria of function, 90
Prescriptions, including norms,
Problem orientation, 4, 34ff
Procedure, principles of, 15, 39
Professional identity and training, 112ff
Professions, defined, 12
Projection, as problem orientation, 53ff

Promotion outcome, 29
    criteria of function, 88
Propaganda, 26
Prototyping, distinguished from experimentation and intervention, 70
Public order, 1

Qualifications of policy scientists, 137

Rectitude value, 43
Respect value, 42
Ruml, Beardsley, xii

Science, in policy sciences, 2, 49
    oligarchy and militancy, 122
    highly capitalized, 124
    visibility and vulnerability, 125
    current proposals by scientists to
        scientists, 126
    like everybody else, 127
    and cognitive maps and procedures,
        128
    common vs. special interests of, 130
Scope value, 3
Shared power as goal, 44
Signs, 26
    as bits, 55
Situations, classified, 25
Skill value, 43

Social process model, 15ff
Strategy, of policy sciences, 61, 63
Strategies, 26
Symbol specialists, 11
Symbols, 26, 55

Termination outcome, 29
    criteria of function, 92
Training, professional, 132ff
    context and specialty, 134
    centers, departments, schools, 136
    qualifications, 137
    integration of training components,
        140ff
Trends, historical, 9, 48
Trust, problem of, 79ff

Ur-Nammu of Ur, 10

Value, list of eight terms, 18, 42
    indulgence and deprivation, 20
    investment and enjoyment, 22

Watson, James D., 3
Wealth value, 42
Well-being as preferred goal, 42
World Government, 30
    polarity, 30